LAST 2 DOLLARS
The Bountiful, Copius, Plenty.

A Guide to Everything You've Ever Wanted.
*A radically different view on wealth,
how to attain it and maintain it!*

GENO BRADLEY, MBA

All Rights Reserved. No part of this book may be reproduced or transmitted in any form or any manner, electronic or mechanical, including photocopying, recording or by any information storage and retrieval system, without permission in writing from the author (or) publisher. Please direct all inquiries to info@ellisandellisconsulting.org.

Published by:
Ellis & Ellis Consulting Group, LLC
www.ellisandellisconsulting.org
242-347-2347 / 678-438-3574

Copyright © 2015. Geno Bradley, MBA
Isbn-13:978-1511922432
Isbn-10: 1511922435

DEDICATION

My Motivation

      This book is dedicated to my partner in crime. She is my parenting partner, the mother of my daughter, (my princess). Latrisa is my business partner and my partner in life. My wife and I met when we were in the 3rd grade in 1986, so although we have only been married 17 years, we have been a part of each other's lives for almost 30 years. Our marriage has been a roller coaster ride that was well worth the price of admission. To my wife **Latrisa "Cookie" Bradley**; I love you and this project is for you. They have created TV characters to "try" and create someone like the woman I have. Thank you for your encouragement to complete the project. Thank you for coming up with the title of this book. Like I told you back in 1992, I just want to take care of you.

My Future

      To my daughter, **Rasheema Bradley**. You represent the absolute best parts of your mother and I. You are The Bradley's love child. My love and support for you has no end. You are the future. I have all of the hope in the world for the woman that you will become. I pray that God keeps you and protects you as you grow.

My Family

To my mother Joyce Fortenberry and my Stepfather Larry Fortenberry (RIP) along with the rest of my family in Mississippi, Georgia, Virginia, Florida, & Minnesota; I will never forget where I come from. I will never forget Miller Street, The North End, My Auntie Trish, Aunt Ree, and my Grandma Miss Joyce Ann. I will never forget the family that raised me, loved me and respected me before I had ever accomplished anything, I love you all.

My Church Family

To my Pastors and spiritual parents; Pastor Nick Travitt & Dr. Rhonda Travitt: Thanks for the push. *I love you guys.* You have helped to bring out the best in me. *Iron sharpens Iron.* I hope that you guys are pleased with what I have produced. It is important to the student that the master is pleased with the work. Thank you for teaching me and thank you for providing me with a safe place where I am free to worship God. To the rest of my church family at Restoring the Years Global Ministries, thank you for your love. I will give my very best effort to love you all the way that God intended.

I also want to extend my thanks to Pastors Paul & Davena Ellis and the team at Ellis & Ellis Consulting Group for being such an excellent partner for my enterprise. You guys are awesome! Thank You for making this dream a reality.

CONTENTS

	Prologue	6
	Writer's Intent	10
	Letter to the Reader	11
1	Wake Up – *Key 1 Wisdom (Understanding Wealth)*	12
2	Blueprint for the Good Life- *Key 2 Reciprocity (Giving)*	47
3	Got Skills? – *Key 3 Competency*	57
4	Popes and Superstars – *Key 4 Strategy*	87
5	Ready, Set, Go! – *Key 5 Operation (Action Oriented)*	103
6	The Pencil Sharpener – *Key 6 Infinity*	110
7	A Servant's Heart – *Key 7 Humility*	119
8	It Matter's How We Win! – *Key 8 Integrity*	129
	Epilogue-*What was this all about?*	133
	End Notes	137
	About the Author	138
	GBC Wealth Index	139

:PROLOGUE

By Latrisa Bradley, RDH

Geno and I grew up extremely different. Even though we went to the same middle school and high school, lived in the same town, and knew many of the same people, our lives were totally different. I was a very sheltered child with the whole world at my fingertips, while Geno was not. In the beginning it appeared as if everything was always given to me and he had to work so hard to attain just the basics. Well, that's how it was at FIRST. It "seemed like" (to everyone else) as soon as I married Geno I immediately became poor, because there was no more luxury, no more fancy cars, life got real... And guess what??? I never noticed...to me it was one of the wealthiest times of my life... Why is this???

Could the answer be that I was dumb and didn't want to face reality, perhaps he was just so good looking that a monthly income of 700 appeared as 7,000.... Nah.... I was totally in LOVE and money never mattered. I was WEALTHY.... I had love, love, love.... I have heard that LOVE don't pay the bills... but guess what LOVE pays mine. It always has and always WILL... I define wealth as LOVE... I define LOVE as GOD as He so loved the world he gave his only son John 3:16. Love endures long and is patient and kind, love never is envious 1 Corinthians 13:4.... Naturally to me.... *#Love* is providing for family, loyalty, compassion, always and forever forgiving, listening with understanding, communicating, joyful, humility. Through sacrifice and commitment to each other God has always allowed us to have more than enough. As we grew in Christ our wealth (love) grew, as we increased our prayer life our marriage became stronger; as our faith increased we were able to accomplish and overcome all different types of stressful obstacles. Geno and I have two different perspective about wealth however, our decision on what we do with our last two dollars are the primarily the same.

My natural father Wayne D. Wilson did not have a college education but he still managed to become wealthy! He worked 80-120 hours a week like a 40 hour work week. He made wise investments in the stock market and had hundreds of thousands of dollars in real state by the time we was 40. He soon retired at 47, he became a stay at home dad, raised his 3 year old daughter (me) while he financed his wife's education. Momma went on to complete her education and achieved a Specialist Degree in education. .. What an excellent example of a wealthy dad.

He sacrificed and I am proud to say I DON"T HAVE "DADDY ISSUES"… naturally and definitely not spiritually either. WHO does that? Only the Father… His Son… and Our Keeper (Holy Spirit)…But God Blesses the child who has his own… and YES HE HAS. I had an extremely wealthy childhood. NOT because of money, it was because I had two loving parents who cared for me and sacrificed on my behalf (priceless). Needless to say, now I am married to a future millionaire now, but I am a future millionaire too and it has nothing with money and everything to do with my bloodline and being a joint heir with CHRIST…I have experienced what very few girls and women will ever experience… Real LOVE from 2 parents, a 3P husband (priest, provider, and protector) and the love of a child. Back in the day Geno said…. Latrisa…. you are going to give the house away. The more I make…. the more you give away…. That's Right boo….

Let's fast forward 18 years. This book simply entitled *Last Two Dollars* will surely get your wheels turning and spark flames. What would you do with your last couple of bucks? How would you invest it? Or hang on to it? Even though Geno I have somewhat of a different perspective on wealth we still flow on the same page. How can two walk together unless they agree? (Amos 3:3).

If you are reading this book to learn how to get rich quick go ahead a stopping reading it and burn it now. This book gives real strategies and maneuvers' to enhance growth at any age. ###Warning!!!!… Geno is extremely rough and cut throat. This book is not for sensitive or pitiful folks. This book will probably make you feel some type of way. It may seem cold, but, it is his truth. Remember we grew up on opposite sides of the tracks. I pray that you are or will become motivated to mix faith and action together and make our own secret sauce….For HIS Glory.

8 KEYS

The Wealthy House

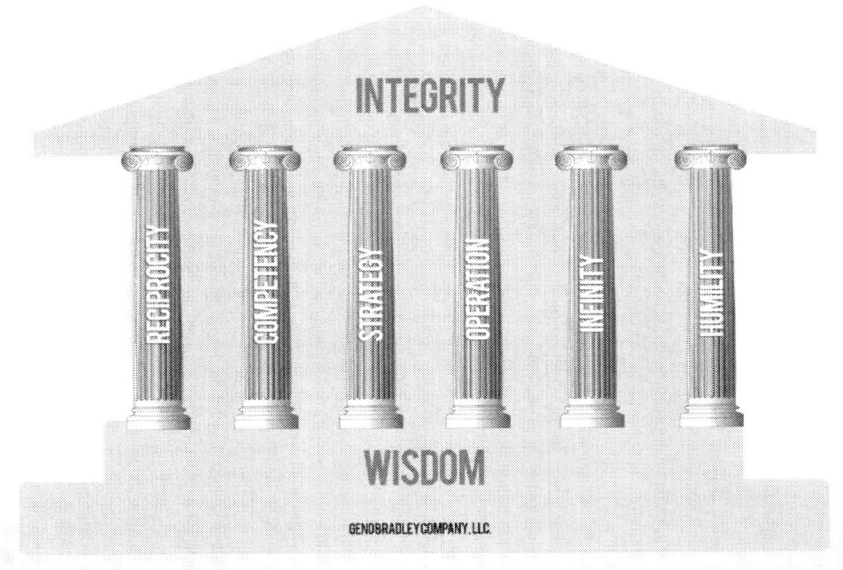

For more information Geno Bradley Co. visit us online:
www.genobradley.com

:WRITER'S INTENT :

From the Desk of Geno Bradley, MBA

Thank you for selecting this book. I pray that you enjoy the material and that you learn at least one thing that you didn't already know. Furthermore, I pray that the material leaves you feeling inspired into executing the great plans and ideas of your own that you have been waiting to share with the world. This is a very modest goal, but statistics have proven that most people don't retain very much of what they read. Maybe something that is said in this book become a lasting memory that sticks with you for years and that you return to this wealth plan to review the material. With God's blessings I am confident that you will have a clear understanding of the core content which is a strategy for life, *not just finances.*

It is plain and simple; this is a book about *wealth*. It is about "Understanding, identifying and __*then*__ Gaining Wealth" and using it for a purpose. It is about making wealth last and more importantly, it is about giving away as much of it as you can (reciprocity). I stand firmly on these principles, and not only are these principles currently advancing my life, but they have been proven to be guiding principles for some of today's most "successful" (wealthy) people. One of the most important paradigms that we will discuss in the book is that wealth comes in many forms. *Are you ready, let's go!*

:DEAR READER :

All of the information is relevant in today's business world but it is scripturally based. The true essence of this book is to simply provide an inspiration that sparks a fire deep inside of every reader to *"Go Hard"* for the Kingdom; or would you rather for the Kingdom be sick & sad, with crusty faces holding our hands out for a donation. When I speak of Kingdom, I am speaking both literally and figuratively. I am referring to both The Kingdom of God, to which we are apart as the body of Christ, but I am also referring to our own part within the Kingdom. This includes our homes, the things we control and the lives that God has blessed us with. Some believe that poverty is a form of humility, but that is a lie that has been inserted into the world's belief system to keep people from aspiring for success. In this book we will explore that lie and many other factors that influence wealth. We will also delve into what the Bible says about that very elusive subject.

KEY 1: WISDOM
Wake-Up

LAST TWO DOLLARS

If you only had two dollars left to your name. It is all of the money that you have, and you have no job, so there is no paycheck coming. As a matter of fact, it might be even more serious to imagine that you had no money left and you borrowed the two dollars. Either way, you only have 2 bucks. What would you do with it? Write your answer below. Don't think on it too long. *What is the first thing that comes to mind?*

> If you want to measure real growth, evaluate the depth of pain that you are feeling in the process.

WEALTH

When you mention the word wealth, everyone immediately thinks of money. Having money is good and it is also one very important aspect of being wealthy, but that is not all there is to it. Money has been at the center of the hunt for wealth since the beginning of time. Even cavemen had an understanding of value and equity. I may refer to the words value and equity often as they are critical in describing what wealth is.

In the caveman era, each person that survived had eventually learned the skills required to make food, clothing, and shelter. These individuals wouldn't have needed money because it had never been spoken of and they did not yet have a need for it. Each family was self-sufficient at hunting, making clothing, cooking, making shelter etc. But it doesn't take long for people to understand that it was unpleasant and possibly even deadly to go without the things that were needed. How could the dollar bills made of cotton have helped them? How could coins have helped them? How about the gold that our currency is based on? An arena full of gold bars wouldn't have helped them either.

WEALTH, WISDOM, KNOWLEDGE

I have had debates with people over the differences between wisdom and knowledge and which is more important. I have also been argued down by people that attribute knowledge as something evil. It is not. Some have placed a dark cloud around knowledge as if it were a plague. Knowledge has also been equated with arrogance. Do not allow people to put you down because you seek to better yourself and improve your life through knowledge. Leave the pretend, wannabe, modest heroes to wallow in his or her ignorance and let them call it wise. If people choose not to learn, it is their prerogative. Is knowledge evil? Of course it is not. Don't be silly. Can we not have wisdom and knowledge? Here is what the Bible says about knowledge.

- **Proverbs 18:15** - An intelligent heart acquires knowledge and the ear of the wise seeks knowledge.
- **Proverbs 2:10** - For wisdom will come into your heart and knowledge will be pleasant to your soul.
- **Hosea 4:6** - My people are destroyed for a lack of knowledge
- **Proverbs 8:10** – Take my instruction instead of silver, and knowledge rather than choice gold.
- **Proverbs 24:5** – A wise man is full of strength and a man of knowledge enhances his might.
- **Proverbs 10:14** - The wise lay-up knowledge, but the mouth of a fool brings ruin near

Nowhere in that text did God say that knowledge was evil. Knowledge gets a bad rap because there are **_some_** intelligent and knowledgeable people that become puffed up because of the knowledge that they have. This is the result of a lack of humility to go along with the knowledge. Wisdom is required to know when to put your knowledge to use and when to keep quiet. If you are among people that don't read, won't learn and despise knowledge, you will make enemies by showing them what you know, even if what you know can help them. *It is better to keep quiet among fools. It is not wise to push knowledge onto those who do not respect it.*

So what exactly is wealth? Is it money, is it fame is it popularity? Is it the power to control our own life, or is it the power to control others? Is it wisdom or knowledge that we need? Or is it both? Dictionary.Com defines wisdom and knowledge as:

"Wisdom" (Noun)

- the quality or state of being wise; knowledge of what is true or right coupled with just judgment as to action; sagacity, discernment, or insight.
- scholarly knowledge or learning:
- *the wisdom of the schools.*
- wise sayings or teachings; precepts.
- a wise act or saying.
- Wisdom of Solomon.

"Knowledge" (Noun)

- acquaintance with facts, truths, or principles, as from study or investigation; general erudition:
- *knowledge of many things.*
- familiarity or conversance, as with a particular subject or branch of learning:

- *A knowledge of accounting was necessary for the job.*
- acquaintance or familiarity gained by sight, experience, or report:
- *a knowledge of human nature.*
- the fact or state of knowing; the perception of fact or truth; clear and certain mental apprehension.
- awareness, as of a fact or circumstance:
- *He had knowledge of her good fortune.*
- something that is or may be known; information:
- *He sought knowledge of her activities.*

While Knowledge is important, it is not the most important factor. As you can see from the definitions above that knowledge is a familiarity or awareness, gained from experience. Head knowledge and book sense is carnal. It is exposure to new materials, mediums and memorization of functions and the results of choice and action through practice. I appreciate knowledge and it is awesome to have this experience and it is oh-so very necessary in the execution of our work, but wisdom is a state

> *For Wisdom is a defense, and money is a defense: but the Excellency of knowledge is, that Wisdom gives life to them that have it.*
>
> Ecclesiastes 7:12

of mind. It is from above. It is all up to you. Would you like to be wise and poor? Wise, in simple matters, but unlearned to the work that is to be done or the skills required for doing the work. This is the poverty that comes along with being in the wrong profession, or never learning to master a profession, never learning to master a craft. This kind of poverty is caused, by not knowing what you want to be when you grow up. It comes from delaying your own learning because for so many years, you have despised the knowledge and ability of others due to your own jealousy. Could one with knowledge become wise? Could one with wisdom gain knowledge? We have to stop allowing people that don't have both, talk down on the element that they don't have. We have to stop letting people who are against learning spend time around us and our children. Our children are the ones trying to make up their minds what they will become. The more you allow them to sit and listen to people that bash knowledge, the more your children are influenced. They will have you and your children thinking that knowledge is bad and you will eventually find yourself in a tax bracket, or a statistical grouping that you do not want to be in. You may find yourself envious of people who are winning at life. What exactly is winning? Remember that question? You want to be wise and poor. It depends on the individual and what they value. Gain Wisdom and Knowledge because, that place where wisdom and knowledge converge is *the sweet spot*. You determine how much knowledge, wisdom, and skill you need for your life! There is not a one size fits all solution to this. The level that is good for you and your family may be different from what I have chosen for my family. The key is not to judge one another based on the lives we have chosen for ourselves. I won't judge you because I don't have a heaven, or a hell, or a jail to put you in, so don't judge me!

COLLEGES & UNIVERSITIES

Anyone who knows me knows that I am a big proponent of the American college and university system. I will take this time to send a big shout out to my fellow Saint Leo University, Kennesaw State University, & Mississippi State University graduates. I truly believe that the knowledge that is gained through the college process is very valuable, but bear in mind it takes wisdom to make the choice to attend college. It is a wise choice to go to college. So does that mean that the person was wise before they went to college? Of course! To a certain extent it takes wisdom to discern whether college is a good decision or not. It is wise to attain knowledge; however, college is not the only place where this knowledge can be attained. Seek wisdom it packed full of all sorts of knowledge.

Wisdom is required in order to make the proper use of knowledge. Ever heard the old saying "book smart, with no common sense"? Well this is proof of the critical value and nature of wisdom. It takes wisdom to put knowledge to use and to use it in the appropriate time and application. This is how people end up going to school and graduating with a degree, certificate, or a diploma and never putting it to use. They may have lacked the *wisdom* for its application.

During the 2015 *"Black Girls Rock"* honors, Michelle Obama, Lawyer, First Lady of the United States of America addressed the TV and the live audience about the importance of getting an education. She referred to the things that the girls needed to do in preparation for a life and career. The thing that she really drove home with the girls is that education was the most important action that you can take for your future. She went on to say that education was the reason that she had made it to the place where she was today standing on that stage addressing the girls as The First Lady of The United States of America and the highest ranking woman in the Free World.

Wisdom is knowledge from above. It is what King Solomon possessed. King Solomon didn't go to the University! But, If King Solomon was here today, I am sure He would advise high-school graduates to go to college to give them a better chance at life. But like I always say, *"No Heaven, No Hell, No Jail"*. If your plan is to tell your children not learn through the college and university system, then that is on you. Good luck with that! But for those who just can't go that route, life is not over. There are numerous career opportunities that can be attained outside the classroom. Ensure your kids have the right mentors to assist them along the way. It's no insult to you, but you may not be the best career mentor for your children. Maybe, Maybe not!

BEYOND MONEY

I know that when you bought this book you may not have thought we would be exploring these types of topics. You may have imagined that it would only cover how to earn more money how to be more productive, how to make your money last longer, how to protect it and other financial topics. We are going to cover those topics in detail however it is my intent to drive home the point that there is a lot more to wealth than just money. My ultimate goal is to change, or add to your perspective. My focus is the personal philosophy, perspective, and the definition of wealth. I hope that I don't disappoint you by saying that this book is actually not about money! Wealth is much greater than that. Decide for yourself.

HEALTH

How about health, wellness, and peace of mind? What about family, freedom, independence, and entrepreneurship. How about salvation? How about those things? Let's talk about the principle of healthcare just for a second. When a parent has a sick child they will do just about anything to make that child well again. So, I personally rank health very high on the scale of the things that we equate with wealth. What about a healthy marriage or healthy business, or even healthy career? Back in 2006 I had finally made a transition into a senior management job. I was ecstatic about the new opportunity and the fact that I would be earning more money and my family was happy about it as well. The opportunity was more exciting than the pay.

Since then my wife has also took another step deeper into her Dental Career. My mother-in-law, was very happy with where we were and where we were headed with our careers and she had a totally different perspective than we did. She was happy for us that our careers had started to blossom and also very happy to know that her daughter and her granddaughter would be well taken care of. What she said to me next changed my perspective on things they gave me a totally different paradigm to work from and I thank her for it. She said *"well son and daughter, you guys have that part taken care of now please make sure that you go to the doctor and get your physicals and keep your health in order so that you can live long enough to enjoy it."* This may sound very simple however in today's society with fast moving careers and people moving from house to house all the time with lots and lots of appointments and places to travel and eating fast food and getting very little sleep these days; I can see how America has become so unhealthy. Health is one of those things that you take for granted until it is gone.

If you had just hit the lottery; imagine how would you feel. Would you be thinking of how your mind would be racing and making plans of all of the things that you would do with your new found wealth. All of the places that you would travel, all of the things that you would buy, all of the clothing and houses, and maybe you might even be generous enough to have a list of people that you would like to give money to. You may want to donate money to your church. Maybe buy a few cars. Maybe buy a new home. Now imagine that you have been diagnosed with an in-operable brain tumor. At that point, the money would mean nothing to you, because you would pay any amount of money to become well again and to make the tumor go away; Especially, if the doctor tells you that it is an impossible operation and it has a 100% fail rate to try and operate to remove your tumor and you would surely die and advises you not to do surgery because it is impossible.

For someone that is immobilized due to a problem with their legs, the ability to walk without pain is very important. Important enough to pay anything to make this problem go away and get back to normal. This is why knee replacement and hip replacement surgery is so popular and also why it is so profitable. People need the service and they are willing to pay. Surgeons are willing to do the work to sell the service. What's important to the doctor is different from what's important to the patient, but they need each other. This is the same for Lupus, Sickle Cell Disease, Leukemia and other chronic Diseases that have treatment, but no cure.

I have survived a few car accidents. I am eternally grateful to God for keeping me in one piece. The last car accident that I was in, was the worst. It was the snow and ice storm of February 2014. Here in metro Atlanta, Georgia we were completely unprepared for what was headed our way. During this time, I am an Operations Manager at a manufacturing facility, and this caused me to take great care and effort to get everyone of our associates out of the building and on their way to their homes in time. I organized meetings with the other Management team members, executed the plan and I ensured that I was the last person to leave the building. This is what leadership is. I am honored that these people were placed under my charge and to that I am responsible for their safety. I left the plant that day driving my big, pretty pickup truck, (that I had very much enjoyed). I merged onto the expressway and I hadn't been traveling for even 1 mile when I lost control of my vehicle because of the ice and started drifting off of the road. I had the experience that so many speak of where your life flashes before your eyes in a millisecond. I smashed into the guard rail, bounced off and then the vehicle swung around end over end down I-75 for a little ways until I smashed into the guard rail a 2nd time and then finally coming to a stop with half of my vehicle on the median and the other half in the right lane of the expressway. I was a little frazzled, but not hurt. I had to quickly get it together. I cannot sit and whine and complain, or wait for a rescue, because there were vehicles headed right towards me down I-75 and I am still in the road. It's important for me to keep things in perspective. I eventually made it home, my vehicle was a total loss, but I got out without a scratch. I didn't let very many people know what happened, so I didn't get a lot sympathy. No one knew. It was important to me to depend on God and the thank Him for my safety and to be sure that I didn't turn the attention of my friends, family, and my church to me. I felt that there were so many other people and their situations that needed help. God Got me. I was fine.

The accident gave me a different perspective on life. I am not waiting for a diagnosis, or the next crisis to enjoy life. I have started crossing items off of my bucket list immediately.

Funny how I only told a few people what happened, but the only thing people ever ask me is "what happened to your truck"? It is a miracle to get out of a vehicle that is a total loss, but the nature of man is to think about **_stuff_**. No one ever asked if I was ok. This is why I decided not to tell anyone else. The victory belonged to God. My new perspective makes me no longer spend time doing things that I am not passionate about. Why waste my life on things that are not priorities. Similar to the Philosophy of Steve Jobs, I only work on stuff that is important to me. This list of places that I want to travel to and the things I want to do. I am getting them all done now.

I lost a friend at a very young age and learned the same valuable lesson from Barry Pearson. Barry and Tammy Pearson were one of the few couples (outside of family) that my wife and I befriended after leaving the military. When I am ready to switch gears, or get some rest, I will always say to my wife: "If Barry could come back to life, I am sure that he wouldn't be racing his car to get in line with the traffic on the expressway to go to a job. He was an ordained Minister, but I am not sure that he would be racing to church for a corporate worship experience either. In church with his boys in one room, wife in another room busily working to serve is not where Barry would be headed. He would race to his wife and to his sons. Barry wasn't perfect. No man is without fault, but he loved his family; and I love mine. They may not understand or appreciate my love for them just in the same way that at times I have taken their love for granted. They don't know that I pray over my wife and my daughter and anoint my home with oil early in the morning before they rise. They may or may not know that I intercede for them every single day that I wake. More reverence is paid to the man with the microphone that is praying with band playing behind him and 10 speakers blaring loudly. I will continue to express my love and my duty to them. I am the priest, provider, and the protector. I will lay down the offense that is felt when they say to me that "so and so" prayed a mighty powerful prayer for me and the ladies today. I will pray while they rest. It is the same way that we take the air that we breathe for granted, yet we complement each other's clothing and cars and other worldly trinkets and probably do not thank God enough for our lives.

I am an extremely busy Business Executive involved with many organizations and professional projects, but they all fall in line, behind my family. So the time that I am available is either good enough or it is not good enough. Period. I don't have to protest or cause a fuss to get the time off that I need. I just balance my schedule based on what my family needs first and then my associates must understand and schedule around, "The Bradley's" schedule. I am not being selfish I am just putting my family first. After all, if it had not been for that guard rail, I would have been gone. Thank you Lord.

At this point I would ask that you indulge me for a moment. If this was your situation what would you rather have, the money and 45 days to live, or would you rather have a healthy body and a long life where you live to see 100 and healthy enough to travel and spend time with your children, grandchildren, and great grandchildren to see them all grow up. I know which one I would choose. *How about you?*

PEACE OF MIND

Now let's talk about peace of mind. This is something that cannot actually be bought with money. Money can possibly help you to establish temporary peace of mind based on the security that you purchased for yourself; the security guards that you purchase to protect you, and the taxes that you pay to the government for the police; the mortgage that you paid for your home; and the tuition that you pay for your children; the money that you pay in utilities so that you can be comfortable in your home; however this is not all there is to peace of mind.

Has your heart ever being gripped with fear? Ever thought you lost your kid in the grocery store or the mall? Every parent has probably felt this at some point no matter how good of a parent you are. The feeling of that brand-new little baby that you have that won't stop crying and has a fever, so now you're getting nervous. At this point you will pay anything to have it fixed; However the doctor tells you that you just need to continue to give the baby fluids and a little bit of fever reducer and wait it out because there is no real treatment for a baby with a fever. The parents are immediately nervous and anxious and waiting and praying that nothing happens to their child.

Sometimes these episodes turn out to be minor and your child heals up in just a matter of days and just like that just as quickly as it came it's gone and the baby as well. And also just as quickly as your heart was gripped with fear and you lost your peace of mind you have gained it back just that quickly and oh how quickly we forget about the suffering that we were just in a day or two before.

Everyone has heard the stories of parents leaving their children in the car all day while they are at work. I am no better than any of them. I have felt the simultaneous pain and relief of pulling into the parking lot of my job and then hearing my 6 month old on the back seat. I wanted to shout for joy that I had noticed and the problem and avoided the mistake and at the same time saddened with the thought that I could have made a fatal error. I don't judge the folks in the news, because it could have been me. One mistake could have cost my daughter her life. I thank God for stepping in. The moments leading up to this were peaceful. Easy drive, listening to the radio and then panic, chaos, horror sets in and my heart almost stopped. I am wealthy. I am blessed.

Security also brings peace of mind to most people. No one wants to live in a neighborhood where there are constant crimes of robbery, rape or shootings or any other kinds of violent crimes and typically we all do whatever we can to get ourselves into the best neighborhoods that we can. We also go through great efforts to get our children into the best schools that we can. But if you think about it we are a bit selfish in that respect because we are mainly concerned about our own home, subdivision and communities. We are so focused on our child's school that we are often times guilty of having no thought of the surrounding areas in our metropolitan or, what is happening in the rest of our city / state, or what is happening in the rest of our country, or what is happening around the globe. Most of the time people think that the things that are happening outside of their immediate area are not going to affect them but that is so wrong. The battle between the haves and the have-nots could easily end up at your front door.

Never forget about the Prisoners of War, (POW's) that were taken and abused for your right to drive around free here in America.

Men and women died and some were tortured for the freedom of America. All so that Americans can complain because it takes the food too long to come out at the restaurant. All so that Americans can still look at other with their nose in the air, because they believe that some people of certain racial and economic status are better than others. Men died so that what we could do with our freedom is; to hate each other, kill each other and complain about what we want the government to do for us. Give me a check, make it bigger and although you built these nice roads for us, and installed the guard rails to keep us safe, "it could have been better".

Never forget the bodies that were snatched and sold into the sex trafficking business. Never forget those that were raped and left for dead. Girls, women and boys have been taken for years and most are never heard from again. This is modern day slavery. If you are walking around free, not enslaved in sex camp, be thankful. Don't judge.

Never forget the man on life support. What is wealth to him? What is wealth to his wife while his fate is being decided? I spent some time with my Stepdad Larry Fortenberry this spring as he lay on a hospital bed, with his life being supported by the machines that hum and beep in the background. Very important to me that I take heed to the lessons that I learned through time I spent with him. I want to take a moment to represent him and to thank him for the good bad and the ugly. I learned from all of it.

Never forget those enslaved by the justice system, locked away for crimes that they didn't commit. Some doing time for crimes that they did actually commit. If you are walking around free, be thankful. Don't judge. Never forget those addicted to drugs who have become someone different altogether because of the stronghold that the drug has on their mind. If you are walking around free with no substance abuse problem, be thankful. Don't judge.

My family and I attend a church where we pray for America often because we understand the principle of peace and we understand the principle of how one community affects another. Just like a wildfire can spread in the forest so quickly that you cannot escape; riots and warfare and crimes against humanity can also spread very quickly as well, so I encourage the people I meet to; at all times be mindful of the state of the union, the state of your community, outside of your community, the community of the human race and the human family. Pray for them, donate to charities get involved give back at homeless shelters, donate money to causes that fight diseases before a deadly virus breaks out and wipes out an enormous population in America because not enough people got involved and not enough people donated money to the societies that are created to fight the spread of diseases. Or because not enough people decided to give back to the homeless shelters and donate food and give out blankets in the world becomes worse and worse over time and just like the wildfire that is spread very quickly violence and anarchy starts to spread. Where would your peace of mind be then? I also rate peace of mind very high on my list of things that I consider to be wealth. *Would you agree?* **Everything is fine, until it's not!**

PERSPECTIVE

A person's perspective is typically going to be shaped based on where they are actually positioned in life. Position equals attitude. What is attitude? Well attitude is really just your position at the time. The proper definition for the word is actually "position."

Every airplane has what is called an "attitude indicator". It is a round ball that is half white on the top and half black on the bottom the ball also has lines on it that tells the pilot what the plane's attitude is. Without this it would be impossible to fly an airplane and keep it level. When the plane turns left the ball starts to rotate so that the pilot and flight crew will understand the actual position in the air. When the pilot banks right or when the pilot drops the nose of the airplane to land it does the same function. This is so that the pilot will always know the physical position of the airplane.

Hate TV commercials? I am easy to please. I don't watch much TV, but when I do I very rarely see a program that I complain about. I have really not complained about bad acting or a bad story. After spending time in "The United States Marine Corp" and having so many months without TV, when we return to "The States", we will watch anything, after I haven't seen American TV for a year. Even the commercials seem interesting. If you complain about TV, you probably watch too much TV. Relax, because your life is too easy. "You don't have any problems unless you don't wake up". (Larry Fortenberry).

Peoples perspective on everything in life has a great deal to do with how you were raised, where you went to school, where you went to college, what your parents do for a living, how you were raised, where you went to church, what you eat, and read, and how much education you have. People who worry about money all the time usually never have any money. Worrying won't make the money stretch and it won't protect the money that you have. You sit and worry and wonder about it, and that's not healthy. But you can sit and plan and strategize; that on the other hand is healthy activity. There are individuals out there who watch the bank every five seconds and comb over their paystubs for every little deduction; and while that seems like they are being a good steward and being watchful, it just seems petty to me. I don't even look at my paystubs and most of the time I forget that I got paid. I know what you're thinking, "this guy makes a lot of money and that's the reason why he doesn't have to worry and that's why he doesn't look at his paystubs". That is not true. I am not one of those overpaid executives that takes things for granted. I am just not paranoid. I trust the system. (Trust but Verify).

When I join the Marine Corps in 1996 my paycheck every two weeks was $352 per pay period. Talk about peanuts. That's what I got for swearing in to Marine Corps combat training and promising to support and defend the Constitution of United States against all foes: foreign and domestic? $352 that's what I got. I am not bashing the military either because it wasn't long before I started to earn more and I was also promoted and by the time I left a military as an E6 or (Staff Sergeant). My salary was decent. (Not great)

I am also often asked why I did 11 years in the military or military and did not do the other 9 years to retire. It has just as much to do with wealth as anything else in the world. My perspective on wealth is my own as should yours be. Most of the guys that I know in the military always talked about being a family guy. Most military people will tell you, "Family comes first." Many people say this yet they will continue to sign up for new contract where they will be deployed over and over again and be away from the family most of the year.

What I value is time with my daughter very highly. She didn't want me to continue to leave and I didn't want to leave her either. So I did something about it while I was on active duty I was going to school at night. I would repair airplanes all day long. I was either out in the hot sun or in the freezing cold and then in my oily and dirty coveralls I would go across the street to the Saint Leo University campus and take college courses to prepare myself for the future. It was a part of my strategy to ensure that when I left the military I would have more options for work.

Many of my fellow Marines were dedicated family men and women and loved their families very much but their priority was not spending time with them and being with them but the priority was actually providing for them. They would subject themselves to the deployment and be separated from their families many months throughout the year just to make sure that that military paycheck every 1st and 15th kept rolling in. I was guilty of the same thing. At some point military families don't feel confident in their ability to earn a decent income after they get out of the military so they simply stay in and continue on and make that their career.

It is a lucrative career and it is very rewarding but not for me. Being with my daughter comes first. It is just not providing for her that comes first. It is raising her and being with her. I remember one day that it hit me like a ton of bricks. Lots of military people smoking at the time I did too, so we used to go out to the smoking area and there were pull-up bars and places to do push-ups and sit-ups while you smoke. I was out there sitting talking with one of my fellow Marines and he was very concerned about being with his family and he was saddened about the fact that we were planning for a deployment to Afghanistan that was about to take place in less than 60 days. While talking with him it hit me. I didn't marry my wife so that I could leave her and be in a long distance relationship. It was time to renew my contract but I turned down the opportunity and the bonus because I had confidence in my own ability to earn money after I got out and I was motivated by the future. I was motivated to be with them.

I was not one of the service members that was nervous about work in the private sector. I have faith in God to take care of me and I have faith in my own ability to get it done. But also, I didn't just let it happen, there was a purpose behind all of my actions. So while my fellow Marines went to the bars at night and hung out with each other I was in the classroom preparing. The military is a great career, so don't misunderstand what I'm saying. If you are a career military person don't be all butt hurt because my choice is different than yours. Understanding wealth and having key 1, which is Wisdom is the ability to understand what wealth is to you.

GET YOUR PRIORITIES STRAIGHT

People, we need to get our priorities straight in America. It seems that at times it is more important to look a certain way, than it is to take care of our very important priorities. The information that we are putting forth here in this book is not to judge anyone or to condemn anyone. I know better than to judge, but we do need to point out as many of the errors in our lives as we can so that they can be corrected. If you believe in continuous improvement then we have to find a way to make the problems visible so that we can identify them and then solve them.

Learn God's plan for you. Learn the world system. Learn the American system. Make the plan and then work the plan. Learn the laws of the land so that you can stay free. We all take risks, but it is better to take calculated risks than to just blindly jump. Police officers are killing black men throughout America, but don't be fooled. This has happened in every nation since the beginning of time. Why do they kill us? What is it about us that makes nations want to either own us, or kill us? It is Greatness.

Police officers would rather harass people for petty discrepancies like window tint, headlights and taillights. They use these issues to harass people that they don't like (black men). They know what a black man's car looks like. It's the cleanest one on the road with shiny oil on the tires. These cowards love to pull us over and give us tickets for nonsense. No courage to go into the really dangerous places in America and do battle with real crime. I haven't always been the middle class guy that I am today. I have lived in the gutters with the rats. I have been face to face with dirty cops, drug dealers and murderers. I have had a gun put to my head. I have been threatened. I have been jumped. I have been in "the field" and on the street. The police officers are poorly trained and poorly managed. Some of them are corrupt and some are afraid. They won't battle the mob or the mafia. They won't investigate CIA and

FBI killings. They won't go head to head with international drug operations. They would rather shoot down unarmed black teenagers. Cowards.

I have my priorities straight. I am not naive to the fact that when people see me they see talent, power, intelligence, strength, and purpose. I understand that some will embrace me because of it and yet others may attempt to harm me because in their minds, I am a threat. I have analyzed the risk and decided that I will still leap for greatness no matter how many people I make uncomfortable along the way. Be sure you teach your children and your brothers and sisters the law. Be sure to teach them to negotiate the American system so that they can stay out of harm's way. It is insane to do things the same way and expect a different result. Don't keep driving the same direction when you have seen cars going off the cliff one by one, or you will suffer the same fate.

BORROWING MONEY

I haven't borrowed money much in my life but I can't say that I have never done it because I have once or twice. It was a humbling experience and it did not feel very good at all. Maybe it was my pride; or maybe it was just the circumstance; or maybe I just wished that I could've taken care of it on my own. Sometimes it is necessary and I am not here to say that you are evil if you borrow money.

It is just sinful to take your own money and go to the night clubs, and buy beer and cigarettes, and put rims on your car, and go on vacation, and go golfing, and gamble just so that when your bills come around and the important priorities come due; you need to borrow the money. Well now that Facebook is so popular it's one of the things that is helping to get people busted. So it doesn't make me feel very good to see you on vacation on Facebook flying across the country once or twice taking selfies and talking about how much fun you're having and the things that you're buying during your shopping excursions. Especially if you return from your trip and then two days later you need to borrow money. This is not wise.

Because you need to pay one of your utility bills, irresponsible people want to use their own money for fun and to play and go to Dave and Busters, and to buy new clothing, and to buy the things they like, and they would like to borrow the money from the responsible people to take care of the priorities. If you know people like this don't just tell them no, also tell them off! If not, they will continue to do this. Until these people are confronted with their own issues and set straight, they will continue to bounce from person to person taking advantage of people who have their priorities in order. It is a shame if you have an emergency savings and you're saving for college, you're saving for retirement, and you pay your bills on time, but you have withheld a little bit of fun for yourself in order to ensure that the emergency savings was available. But the person who borrows money from you is dressed brand new from head to toe in very nice things and has all the fun in the world. It does not make you a saint if you give away your assets and equity to an irresponsible person it makes you gullible. Wake up!

I find it interesting that there are some people that come to America and don't look for jobs, they open businesses. Asian American households have the highest per capita household income, yet you will rarely see an Asian American working a minimum wage job. They don't work at McDonald's or at the mall. They are split into two main categories. *Category #1:* Come to America and start an enterprise or; *Category # 2*: College educated and working a high paying profession. Same is true for Africans. American colleges are filled with foreigners who understand the value of education, while we have rejected people telling our children that they don't need to go to college. If we don't go, our colleges and universities will continue to be filled with migrants coming to America from India, Caribbean Nations, China, and Africa. That's why all of our doctors are foreign. We have made it next to impossible to complete the Master's and Doctorate degrees that give us the expertise and credentials needed to compete on a global scale. *Wake up!*

It can be unsettling just to think that, the average American cannot attain financial wealth considering the current American Financial system. The Website *Who Rules America.com* illustrates that the top 1% of wealthy Americans have over 40% of the money in the U.S. The top 20% of Americans in respect to wealth, own over 90% of the wealth in the United States.

> *"Money is only the first level and the most basic form of success."*
> *Apostle Dr. Rhonda E. Travitt*

KEY 2: RECIPROCITY (GIVING)
Blueprint for the Good-Life

I can't wait for my tithes to go up! Money is both a popular and controversial topic. For some people, money is easy to come by and for others it is all they think about. While that is true, it doesn't change the fact that some people out there have to fight just to get the basics. The Bradley's have been on both ends of that spectrum. We didn't have much when we were first married, and now we both have been blessed with more. When it comes to money, there are many angles that we could choose to cover. People want to know how to get money. Step up your giving, that is how it's done! For this session, we will focus on *giving*. It is a privilege and an honor to give and my wife and I believe that it is the key to all of the other benefits and opportunities that come from having money. Let us break it down for you.

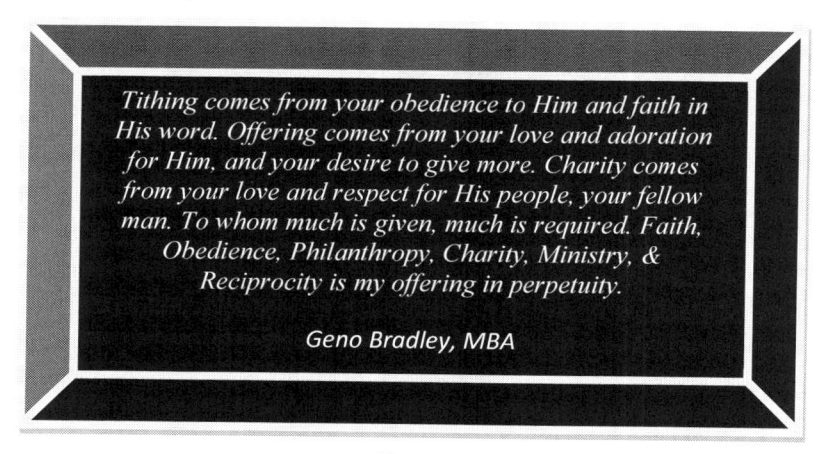

> *Tithing comes from your obedience to Him and faith in His word. Offering comes from your love and adoration for Him, and your desire to give more. Charity comes from your love and respect for His people, your fellow man. To whom much is given, much is required. Faith, Obedience, Philanthropy, Charity, Ministry, & Reciprocity is my offering in perpetuity.*
>
> Geno Bradley, MBA

There are 7 ways to give that will be outlined along with the 3 principles of giving. First the 3 Principles:

3 PRINCIPLES OF GIVING

Principle 1
If you already have wealth and you don't give, your wealth will not last. If you don't have wealth yet and you don't give, you will not attain wealth.
Principle 2
Giving is the opposite of selfishness. God gave His only begotten son. Jesus gave His life. Store up for yourselves treasures in heaven.
Priniciple 3
Giving is the blueprint for wealth.

www.genobradley.com

You must open your hand in order to give from your own hand, but that is also the way that you receive. Imagine your hand closed into a fist. Nothing can be put into your hand, but also you can hang on tightly to what is inside. But if you open your fist, you risk losing what you were holding tightly, but your hand has been opened and in position to receive again. For as long as your hand is open it is always in position to receive. It is in the correct posture to receive.

The People of the world (corporate, entertainers, athletes) already understand this principle and they execute the principle of giving sometimes better than we do inside The Body of Christ. If you don't believe it then do this simple exercise:

1. Close your hand into a fist.
    a. Question 1: can you take anything out?
    b. Question 2: can you put anything in?

2. Open your hand
    a. Question 1: can you take anything out?
    b. Question 2: can you put anything in?

7 WAYS TO GIVE

Before you read this section, I must ask a favor of you. Give me some of your time. Please read the scripture 2nd Corinthians Chapter 9: verses 6-10 before you proceed to read the rest of this chapter. This could refer to money, time, material objects or service to others. God can use me as He desires to fulfill the needs of mankind. The Bible clearly says that through our giving, we will cause men to give thanks to God. People pray. They wait for what they need with an expectation from God. Does God have to come down here do this Himself? Or, will He be pleased with the confidence that through obedience to His word and His plan for us we gave and the others received. We all thanked God.

7 Ways to Give

1. God
2. Family
3. Ministry
4. Charity
5. When Requested
6. Without Notice
7. Support Causes

---

1. GIVE TO GOD

Give back to the God that blessed you with it all.

- Tithes – Do this out of obedience Leviticus 27:30

- Offering – Do this out of Love & Trust – This is giving beyond our ten percent
- Benevolence – Do this to Support the ministry of helps
- Building Fund – Do this to Support the structures that make the worship possible

2. GIVE TO FAMILY

This is where we give to our parents, children and other family members. Some in the Body of Christ give to the church, Pastors, & Apostles, Church Anniversary, Pastor's Birthday, Co Pastor's Birthday, Men's day, Women's Day, benevolence and Building Fund every week……..but wouldn't give a dime to their own family. *That's not holy…. It's just wrong.*

3. GIVE FOR MINISTRY

Giving for your own personal ministry purposes is a good opportunity to spread goodwill. As we travel the Earth for work, school, business and church, we will run into people that will need our help and it will be up to us to take care of it on our own. Be prepared to give, without being asked by the church. The church may never even know what you have done for others, and that is how God prefers our giving to be. Matthew 6:4

4. GIVE FOR CHARITY

We also support public Charities like Must Ministries, American Heart Association, Wounded Warrior Project, and Susan G. Komen etc. These organizations stand for good causes.

5. GIVE WHEN ASKED

This one usually hurts the most. People will catch you off guard, when you least expect it and then ask you to have or borrow something that you were not prepared for. Usually when you give, you have already decided when and how you will give and how much. But when someone asks, we should be ready. Your giving results in thanksgiving to God.

6. GIVE WITHOUT NOTICE

Give without Notice – no plan, just when the Holy Spirit moves you to give.

7. GIVE FOR SUPPORT

Give for Support – Supporting Pastors, Presidential campaigns, People getting together to give a joint gift to someone else. Support other people's projects, ministries, non-profits. Invest into others so that it is easier for organizations to get things done. Supporting Benevolence and Building Funds also fit into this category.

BEWARE OF MECHANICAL GIVING

Beware of "Mechanical Giving". After cookie and I had gotten to the point of being able to give, it became routine. This is not a good thing. God has a way of reminding us that giving should be a sacrifice. When our finances take a hit; the gifts that we have planned to give are a little harder to give. It is here we are reminded that our gifts are truly a sacrifice. If you find yourself in a routine that just seems too easy, here is what you can do:

THIS IS GIVING UNTIL IT HURTS

First-Stop what you're doing and praise God for what you have.
- He has blessed with you with more than enough, so that you can give

Next-Can you give more?
- Be honest with yourself about what you can give, then give until it hurts.
- Be sure your gifts are substantial. Don't shortcut this
- *Remember that this determines what you receive*

Increase your tithes & Offering
- Give beyond your tithes (10%) base
- Give into the offering
- Give into the building fund
- Remember you cannot "outgive God" (Great Return on Investment)

Increase your support of church programs
- Church Outreach
- Benevolence
- Gifts to church members / leaders

Support Local Charities
- Must Ministries
- Homeless Shelters

Support National Public Charities
- American Cancer Society
- Red Cross

Do your own charity
- Help a family in need
- Help your own family (sometimes very difficult)

In summary, this section was about money. These passages are my perspective on money. When I think about wealth, I think of all of the people that I need to help. I think of the resources that can help me to help others. I do not have all of the answers but I enjoy the thought of "My tithes to going up!" You can't give if you don't understand. Once you get it, you can give like never before. Give Back. This is financial wisdom to carry with you for a lifetime:

"If you give until it hurts, you will never be without."
- ***Geno Bradley***

KEY 3: COMPETENCY
Got Skills?

TRADE SCHOOLS VS. COLLEGE

Booker T. Washington & WEB Dubois had different ideas on how disenfranchised peoples can come up out of the depths of poverty. The two men were also very open about their disagreement with the other. Funny thing is that, both of these men were correct. While Booker T. Washington was a strong proponent of Trade Schools and Tech Schools, his counterpart, W.E.B. Dubois, was a staunch advocate of University Degree Programs. These men had open debate about their differences without shooting each other up the way that some of our young people do today to prove a point.

"Let every skillful man among you come, and make all that The Lord has commanded."
Exodus 35:10

I have heard a lot of people that have taking the time out of their day to talk down on college. Most of these people are making a reference to why college is not necessary or how college cannot make you a better person. Some of what they say is correct, but most of it is complete and utter nonsense. The only people who I have ever heard bashing college were people who had never gone to college. Maybe it is jealousy or maybe it is envy for the fact that many people didn't have the opportunity to attend college and some others had the opportunity, but instead they squandered it on partying and socializing and being unproductive because they couldn't make up their mind what they wanted to do with their life.

Many people are also afraid of college. They are afraid that they can't make it, that they are not smart enough, or that they can't complete the work. It is simply not true. They can in fact complete the work but they choose not to. I know many of them. Individuals that I know personally tend not to read because they don't want to learn. College is what you make it. If you want to go, then go. If you don't want to go, then don't go. It is all up to you and your truth. It is about the person you are and the person you want to become. If you do not value what college has to offer then, it is not a part of your wealth strategy. If you want the credentials, but don't want to do the work, or wait; Nowadays you can just buy a degree. It won't make you a better person if you go to college, and it won't make you a bad person if you skip college. That stuff doesn't matter to God. If you want to go, then go, and if you don't want to go to college, don't go. The fact of the matter is knowledge, skills, and abilities are required for certain types of work. Get what you need to get the work done!

If God was not pleased with the laws of the land he would strike them down. He is obviously okay with the governing bodies requiring many years of college and training before you are issued a medical license, or a Dental Hygiene License. You can't just "wish" your way to being a doctor. You have to work your but off in school for many years, and then practice under supervision for many years, before you will be allowed to _apply_ for a medical license. Many other careers have similar criteria. *Be whatever you want to be. Your choice!*

> *"I know people who did not graduate from college that are the most loyal, hardest working, most intelligent and wealthiest people on the face of the earth."*

STEVE JOBS

I have never really been crazy about Apple products but I have found myself recently starting to use some of them. I found that for the most part they are exactly what they were hyped up to be. Founder of Apple, Steven Jobs is one of the people that I have found to be fascinating. What I like most about what I have learned about him is; the fact that he was able to make such a great contribution to history with only a high school diploma. Steve Jobs didn't let people tell him what he could do and what he couldn't do. He didn't allow the fact that he didn't have a degree stop him. He was driven with the motivation from inside to accomplish the vision that was in his mind. Now I am not idolizing Steve Jobs at all, however I believe that we could all learn something from each other including Mr. Jobs.

It is very unlikely that you can be stupid and wealthy. Get skills, go to school, get trained, apprentice under someone else, volunteer, etc. We all need knowledge, skills, and abilities. Delegating everything around to others keeps your skills low. (Sharpen your pencil, get out there and do some work sometime. Even though

Steve Jobs did not complete a college degree, he learned all of it in a college classroom taking only the classes that he found to be useful for creating his company.

With that said I am only trying to bring encouragement to people around the world so that they would understand that university degrees aren't the only way. You could attend a trade school and develop a skill and get a certificate for that skill then go in to the workforce and master your skills to become the best at what you do. You could make a significant contribution to the world as well as provide for yourself and your family. There are dozens of certificate programs out there that take approximately one year to complete. Many of the institutions that provide this level of training also do job placement. You're never too old to go back to school and never too old to learn a new craft.

If you feel like you're getting older and older and your life is passing you by and a four-year degree is simply out of reach. I encourage you to consider one of the trade school programs in your local community or certificate diploma programs at your local junior college or community college. Colleges offer more than just degrees. Most Universities today offer dozens of certificate programs that they typically label under they are continuing education system. Please understand that whether you have developed the skills through 20 years on the job and you have given everything you have towards mastery of your craft, or you went to university system or trade school to have a stamp placed on you saying that you could do this job and then go out into the workforce and prove that you can; either way SKILLS are required. <u>Competency</u> is a must have.

To illustrate this fact one of the requirements that the government uses to screen applicants is to create what is called a KSA file. KSA stands for knowledge skills and abilities. After you have done a long resume and a cover letter and CV and filled out an application online that takes 45 minutes that is still not good enough. With the government will still be looking for in order to judge whether or not you are even worth interviewing is to see what are your knowledge, skills, and abilities or KSA's. There is no place on the application for you to put your Wisdom. Be wise enough to be a productive citizen.

Think about it. Today you will not be allowed to practice law, or medicine. You will not be allowed to build a bridge, or a ship. You will not be allowed to do a laser surgery on someone's eye and you will not be selected to run a company without proof of the skill. You will not be allowed to perform a heart transplant just because you are wise. Without America having these skill sets, The Body of Christ having these skill sets, we will always depend on outsiders to perform these functions. We will be among those who seek outside help for every skill set that is valuable today. Every group of people. Every neighborhood. Every State. Every County. My daughter mentioned that during a research paper for South Africa she learned that the blacks weren't producing enough doctors. Only about 1 in 400. Same thing right here in America, because people are talking down on higher education. This is a dangerous practice.

Skills, Education, Training Matrix

How far can you go in life? Education can get you exposure.

It provides opportunities.

If wealth is at the center, can you reach that core?

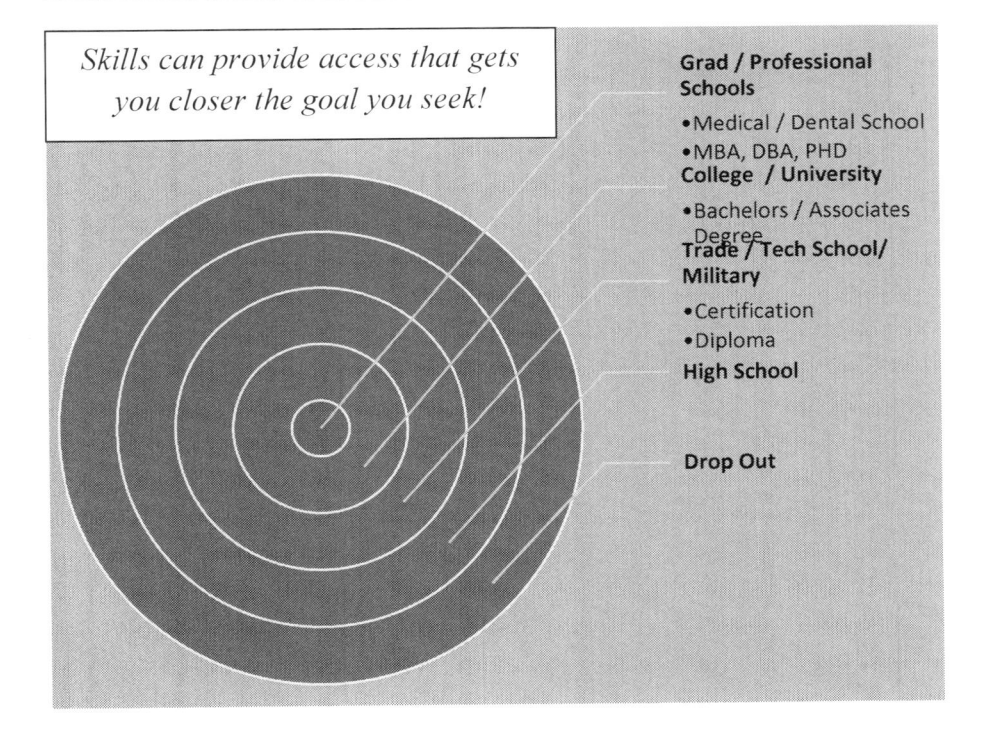

Skills can provide access that gets you closer the goal you seek!

Grad / Professional Schools
- Medical / Dental School
- MBA, DBA, PHD

College / University
- Bachelors / Associates Degree

Trade / Tech School / Military
- Certification
- Diploma

High School

Drop Out

Intelligence and education are two entirely different things. I have often heard people referred to other people and say oh he's so educated. In fact he may be just a high school dropout that has no education at all. That doesn't mean that this person is not intelligent. I have also seen these so-called intellects that have read a few books spent some time in the library and copied the philosophies of other people who did the work to get the information. Many times there are no original ideas, original philosophies or real contributions to mankind.

Intelligence is given to us by God. Education is given to us by men. Each of us has a measure of intelligence that we are born with. I do believe that there are many people that are not college graduates that are highly intelligent. If you were born intelligent then that is who you are. And if you were not born intelligent and there is no amount of college that is going to change that, but we can <u>learn</u>. Everyone can learn. But your IQ (intelligence quotient) will likely remain the same. Your ability to learn and to conceptualize and to create will be the same but you can attain knowledge. Used and maintained properly this knowledge that you can acquire through education can fast-forward you to be competitive or maybe even have an advantage over someone who is simply intelligent, but not formally educated.

Education on the other hand is something that has to be worked for. It has to be earned. The only way to get it is to go through the education system and to have those that rule over the system say when they think that you're educated by issuing you a degree that says that you have completed the requirements for the degree program or the certificate program that you seek.

THE VALUE OF KNOWLEDGE

It isn't even necessary that you be intelligent or highly educated to be wealthy. It all depends on your perspective and how much you want out of life. A person with a mental handicap doesn't want very much in life and they are very satisfied even beyond satisfied with having someone provide for them something that is very simple. People with average intelligence or higher intelligence usually demands much more and are on a never ending conquest to get more. If you value knowledge and you desire to increase your ability and your competency then that knowledge just might be your wealth or a vehicle that helps you to get to your wealth. Remember, The Bible says in Proverbs that my people perish for lack of knowledge. The Apostle Paul says that when I pray, not only will I pray with my spirit but I will also pray with my understanding. If I only pray with my spirit, my mind is unfruitful. In all your getting, get an understanding.

A BIG OBSTACLE: (HUNGRY DOG SYNDROME)

When I was growing up in "the hood" I noticed a few things that stick with me today. Some of the things that I learned that have helped me to learn to treat people with more respect came out of watching the wrong thing happening. I have watched as people would disrespect each other and pull one another down because it appears as if that is a way to bring yourself up. I had to go ahead and give this thing a title because I saw it so much that I needed a way to quickly identify and label this subtle yet widespread evil that was occurring in my neighborhood, my church, my school, my family, my city and my state. Then just as I thought it was just my family I started traveling across the United States and even around the world and I saw the same thing. I was glad to find out that it wasn't just my family that had a few people infected with Hungry Dog Syndrome. It is mental poverty, and it is a global problem.

What is Hungry Dog Syndrome? Well I will try to describe it for you it is when you have people that are so poor growing up and they have such an impoverished mentality that they couldn't possibly imagine giving or sharing. They couldn't possibly imagine being patient with someone because no one has ever shown them patience. These people only receive negativity and hate and they have things taken from them and people compete to take the little bit that they have. This makes a person very aggressive to protect the little bit that they have and it makes you very assertive to go and get more to try to improve your life. This makes you so aggressive and so assertive to the point of being disrespectful to others unknowingly.

Hungry Dog Syndrome will prevent you from sharing and allowing others to share with you because of the rejection that is felt during a dysfunctional upbringing. If it is hard to take a compliment or hard to accept gifts from others, you might be infected.

I had some company at my home once and we ordered pizza and of course people all like different kinds of pizza. But you can see the hungry dog starts to drool and snarl in every situation and every way because they can't help it. So it starts to come out when we decide to pick which kind of pizza and they say well I don't like this, and I don't like that, and I don't eat that, and I only eat this, and they start to show just how very picky they can be at times not knowing that every time you say that I don't eat this and that it could be so disrespectful to the people that do eat those types of food items. It is not good to take such extremes with every decision that you make. It is also not helpful to protest everything. Well I would never do this and I would never do that. Yes you would; If you are subjected to just the right circumstances. So this is something that is just not smart to say. Some of the things that we thought that we would never do we will probably do at some point after we have been exposed or have learned more about the ways of the world. The negativity is just non-productive.

Well as usual for the sake of peace and to be a good host I just decided to order whatever my guests would like and I will just eat that because it's nicer that way. Did I get the kind of pizza that I liked, no? But who cares? Not smart to order a pizza for every person in the house to match their liking. Well we ordered pepperoni and guess what happened next? The pizza arrived and my guest took a slice of pizza and started eating it and noticed a space where there was mostly cheese and started to rant and rave about how they were missing one of the pepperonis! This is Hungry Dog Syndrome.

I have also gone out to restaurants many times with people. I've done big groups are also in small groups I've done really fancy restaurants are done small neighborhood restaurants. I've done five star tablecloth restaurants and I've done hole in the wall taco stands. Either way it is always nice to have someone else cook for you and then serve it to you, bring your plate and to take it away and you can leave the place with a full belly knowing that you have been taken care of. This opportunity that we have in the modern world is something that was not available in the past to people outside of the wealth, nobility and royalty.

Well, nowadays you can be a minimum wage worker and just stroll into a restaurant and someone will show you to your seat and maybe even pull out your chair and they will ask you what you would like to drink and go ahead and bring it to you before any mention of payment or anything happens. It is just a courtesy that the host of the restaurant would get you seated and get you napkins, make sure you like your table, and then offer you something to drink and anything else you would like. They will proceed to go ahead and ask you what you would like to eat and they will go and make it for you right away. Some people with Hungry Dog Syndrome see this opportunity to have **service** as an opportunity to have **servants.**

I have been out with people and watched them terrorize waitresses and waiters to the point of me having to step in and take up for the server. Many of the people that I've seen do this or some of the poorest people I've ever known. You would think that they would have more compassion on a server, but sometimes they can be the worst. It is now their opportunity to inflict the hardship on others that has been inflicted on them. This is Hungry Dog Syndrome

Sometimes they have evil intentions in mind before they even go into the place. The same personality type has also been likely to not want to pay the bill at the end of the service. Of course I will gladly volunteer to pay and will typically reward the server with an unusually large tip to make up for having to accept this type of treatment. You can just about bet they are going to look at the food and frown up their faces at it. It's not going to be hot enough. It's not going to be cold enough. It is not going to have something on it that is supposed to have on it and it is not going to be perfect; and sometimes they send it back. I just don't understand this. But maybe it is just because I am easy to please. *After serving 11 years in the Marine Corps I will eat just about anything as long as it will hold still on the plate.* So when there is a server asking me what they can do for me and they are bringing me really tasty food that is being prepared at a restaurant; I am ecstatic.

HUNGRY DOGS AT WORK

Hungry dog syndrome is also at our workplaces. Have you ever worked with someone that was just 100% negative? These people are never satisfied and there's nothing ever good enough for them. They want the CEOs house and car. They want the boss's paycheck. And they want to run the place, with a GED. Other ways that this shows up is when you have tons of opportunities that come a person's way but they just cannot capitalize on any of them because it is always something that keeps it from being perfect.

Nothing on earth is perfect. You will be waiting a long time and die still waiting on the perfect opportunity. So don't wait on the perfect opportunity, take what is placed in front of you. Seize the moment make the best out of it; make a dollar out of 15 Cents. Hungry Dog Syndrome makes you arrive at work late all the time have a bad attitude, and be rebellious to the leadership of the company.

Everyone wants to be the CEO. But ask yourself this question? Did you do what the CEO did? Did you study and invest at the right time. This is why America is in so much trouble now, because of greed. Skilled and Unskilled laborers demand unreasonable wages. Unions causing businesses to have higher wages only drive factories overseas. This is why we don't make anything in America. The workers want too much. Everything is made overseas because as soon as you hire your work force in your new factory to give the community 2500 new jobs, the next thing that happens is they have a meeting to unionize and then hold the company hostage demanding more and more until the owners decide to make it in Mexico or China. Not worth the trouble. Everyone wants the CEO's paycheck and his house, his car, and his dog. But would you also take the 3-4 times he filed bankruptcy, putting everything he or she had on the line to make this dream possible? Will you live in your car to make this business come alive? Most won't. What these Hungry Dogs will do instead is show up and ask for a job and then demand everything that you have as if they were entitled to it. *That's Hungry Dog Syndrome.*

THE SET UP

People fall for the same trick over and over and over again. But there is no such thing as a free lunch. This is something that we actually studied when I was in undergrad at Saint Leo University. This was actually a part of the curriculum to have us review and study the effects of the appearance of a free lunch. Well I will go ahead and skip to the chase with you and tell you that there is no such thing as a free lunch. Even the time that you spend eating the lunch and taking it from the person who has given it to you is an investment of your time that you could've used to do something for yourself or for your family, but instead you chose to eat free. Lots of people will do anything to get something free or to save a buck. These people also believe that it is better to be careful to only get a certain amount of overtime because they don't want the government to get more taxes. Hungry Dog Syndrome has people believing that paying taxes is a problem. I can't wait to pay $200,000 - $300,000 in taxes. Do you know what that means? That means at the 35% tax bracket (which I don't mind) that means I earned around $1.2 Million. I f your mind is so small that you can't understand "pay to play", le t me help you out. It takes money to make money. Paying taxes is a good thing. Mathematics is our friend ladies and gentlemen.

SPENDING $10 TO SAVE $3

I know people that will drive all over town to save money and get things for the lowest price possible. But it is ridiculous to spend all that gas money and to waste your time. My time is valuable and to me my time is a part of my wealth and I am not willing to invest my wealth into driving around to save just a little. This is also prevalent and even though this is not a smart practice it is okay if this is what wealth is to you and if this is how you want to spend your wealth. Have your way. For some, they enjoy making a good purchase at an excellent price. This is perfectly ok, but I will not allow people to waste my time, so if we are together, (we are not doing that).

So if you're driving yourself to the store and you want to spend $10 in gas driving around town to save 50 cents here and 75 cents there then that is fine but, if I am giving you a ride to the store to a store like Wal-Mart that sells everything in the world, and you better get everything that you can while you're in there, because we're not going down the street to Kroger just because the chicken is a little cheaper; And then you want to go to the dollar store because the toiletries are a little cheaper there. Not on my watch, and I will be rude to you if you ask me to do something stupid like this. If you don't have transportation and then someone offers you a ride then that ride is of great value, it is a form of a gift and gratitude for that gift would be to take it easy on the person that is giving you a ride. People with Hungry Dog Syndrome don't understand this and they will take you for everything that you've got. They won't be happy that you allow them to use your telephone for them to check on their child to make a little bit of peace of mind and relax; they will want to call everyone they know.

They don't just become appreciative of the ability to get groceries to feed their family, now they also need you to stop at the convenient store so that they can play the lottery. They are not just happy that you loaned them $100 …… they will also complain because you didn't give them the exact change. If you really needed $100 to pay something very important for your family right away I am sure that the $98.50 that I gave you will get you pretty close to what you need. These kinds of people would not only complain about being a $1.50 short, but they will also complain that you gave him a check instead of cash. I have literally had people to complain to me because I wanted to give to them, but a check which is more convenient for me is not going to work for them because they want cash. The nerve of somebody to complain like this is Hungry Dog Syndrome.

1964

Throughout history people have not always had the permission or the opportunity to vote and to make decisions about their government. We enjoy that luxury today off of the backs of the men and women who died and were jailed for our right to vote. Now we have a bunch of hungry dogs that are too selfish, too stubborn, and too rebellious to go and vote. A large number of people showed up to vote during the presidential election that elected President Barack Obama to become the first Black President. However, for the Senate race and the governor races around the country that took place in November 2014 there was a much smaller turnout. Voting for Senators wasn't sexy enough to draw out the people. It is just stupid to sit home and complain and to write stupid stuff on Facebook about how the minimum wage needs to be raised but you won't go and vote.

I say if you don't go and vote, then sit down and shut up because you had your opportunity to have your voice heard. There are a lot of conspiracy theories out there also that don't think our votes count anyway and I understand that there are some forces out there that have a lot of control of the world system, but you can't just give up and lie down and allow somebody to spear you in the back with the javelin. If you go out you should go out fighting with the tenacity of a spirit that won't die, and a spirit that won't give up, the spirit that always offers to help, and that always tries to continue to make things better. If not you might as well go ahead and start snarling and drooling with the rest of the hungry dogs.

SKILL SETS

In order to use what's available today, to gain wealth you have to understand and improve your skill sets. You cannot fool yourself into thinking that because you watched Law and Order that you would be a good attorney. How many people do you know the watch something on TV and because they like it they think that they can do it? That's just not true. You need to do a self-check and be sure you understand what your strengths and weaknesses are. Do a SWOT analysis on yourself on your business on your career.

ENTREPRENEURSHIP

I will never be able to say enough about entrepreneurship. It is an amazing experience and an outstanding benefit that Americans have been blessed to have at our disposal. We can't overlook the possibilities, nor can we overlook the fact that other nations do not allow businesses to be formed so easily. We have the opportunity to start a new business everyday if you want to, but "buyer beware".

Don't start with a premature plan. Planning is everything. When a young adult is considering a new career, or when an experienced adult is considering a career change, do not discount the possibility of starting your own business.

American business owners enjoy certain peace of mind from knowing that they are earning money with the company that they have created. Please choose wisely, Business owners are the hardest working people in the world. You will never work as hard as you do when you are working for yourself; working to build your business, working to build a brand, working to survive, because your business making a profit or loss is the difference between your family having groceries or not. Many of the businesses that we drive past each day and many of the businesses where we spend our money each day are not owned by billionaires, or big corporations. They are owned by regular folks, like you and I.

SWOT ANALYSIS

SWOT analysis is an acronym for (Strengths Weaknesses Opportunities and Threats. This is not some textbook mumbo-jumbo this is something that career professionals continuously do and update at least annually.

STRENGTHS

Strength is what is considered to be a core competency. It is something that you're good at, or that you are trained to do, or self-taught and that you do well. It is something you have had success doing and not just in your mind. Real Results. It takes years to master an art or a science. So if you haven't put in the time yet, you haven't invested what it takes, you might want to get started. It is impossible to attain mastery if you bounce around from job to job and career to career trying to figure out what you want to be when you grow up.

WEAKNESSES

We all have weaknesses. Some people will be not be truthful about their weaknesses because they think that acknowledging it exposes them to trouble when it is the exact opposite. When we do not acknowledge our weaknesses, things become very dangerous. If you don't understand what it is that you do poorly, then you cannot ask for help, and you cannot compensate by spending extra time on it and it will end up biting you in the butt.

OPPORTUNITIES

Every opportunity is not for you. You have to understand your strengths and weaknesses before you can decide whether or not an opportunity is a good match for your skill set. As soon as someone comes out with a new pyramid scheme you're the first to sign up for it because it seems like a good opportunity, but business may not be your strong suit. Direct selling may also not be your strong suit. You cannot allow yourself to be thrown around in the wind with everything that people throw at you or, they will have you selling milkshakes, make up energy drinks, coffee, and everything else that people come up with. It seems so easy to doop people into it that you might as well come up with your own. The people who get in early and that are at the top are usually the only ones who make a profit.

If your lifelong dream has been to sing then why on earth would you allow someone to convince you to start selling vitamins and umbrellas? You are now taking away valuable resources and time that could be invested into doing the thing that you want to do most but instead of having an intense focus towards this one important thing it becomes a watered-down effort because you're stretched into too many different places. Really spend time alone and spend time assessing yourself so that you could know who you are and what you stand for and where you are headed. When navigating a ship or an airplane it doesn't take more than just a few degrees off your course to have you wind up in a totally different country. Understanding this will help you to know when the right opportunity comes that, " this is the one for me," and then you can go at it with everything that you have in you.

THREATS

If you are not analyzing the threats to your career, to your business, to your wealth, then you may as well just leave it out on the front porch for anyone to take. The threats for yourself are different from the threats that I have. Every person is different but you need to understand that these threats, (threats to your savings plan, investing plan, business investments, threats to your business, threats to your family, threats to your health), are all threats to your peace of mind. I have been approached on different occasions to go into business ventures that seemed a little shaky and I thank God that I took the time to think about it and sleep on it so that I made the choice not to get involved and not to invest. Thankfully, I also was a bystander when I watched these businesses begin to have problems with the government because they are participating in business activities that were less than best practices.

KEY 4: STRATEGY
Popes & Superstars!

"For which of you, desiring to build a tower, does not first, sit down and count the cost"
Luke 14:28

BASE HITS NOT HOMERUNS

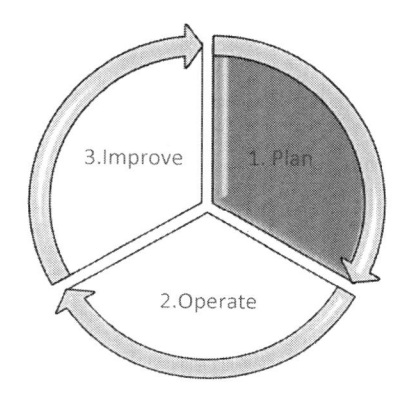

Don't let perfect get in the way of good. Make Incremental improvements. Don't create a plan that is so long and drawn out and so elaborate that you can never get started and you cannot achieve it. We must **Plan** for base hits and not always plan for home-runs. Do you know who Ty Cobb is? Well I sure didn't know who he was either, until I was having a conversation with my coworker Jacob Simpson about a continuous improvement presentation we worked on together. Do you know who Barry Bonds is? Of Course, everyone knows Barry Bonds because he is a big home run hitter. In life we tend to only pay attention to the superstars who make the grand accomplishments. Ty Cobb still holds the record for highest batting average of all time. For 23 years, he held the record for most base hits. He was a valuable player that scored over 100 runs during a season and he did that 11 times. No one mentions him when it is time to talk fancy. Everyone wants a home run.

If you hit a grand slam in baseball then that means there were three people on base and when you stepped up to bat when you hit a homerun and your team got 4 points all at the same time because you knocked the ball out of the park. But many times very little is said about the three players that had to be consistent and concise hitters in order to hit the ball and get on base. Without their efforts knocking the ball out of the park would've only gotten you 1 point and you would've been a very big deal all by yourself. This can be applied anywhere in life. We must play our position and we must continue to do the little things if we want to have a grand success. It takes a team and we must have great people around us in order to accomplish greatness. Getting a base hit doesn't seem like a big deal but it is a very big deal to the guy who keeps striking out and cannot get on base. Getting things done in life is like this. Don't sit around and procrastinate waiting on your grand slam. Don't wait until you can get the perfect job and sit home and wait because you're too good to do certain kinds of work. Don't live in an apartment because you can't afford a one $5 million dollar house. Don't ask for rides and catch the bus because we can't have an S class Mercedes. Make a plan that includes steps, goals, and objectives to get you to the place you want to be in life. Get on base!

Don't sit and stare at the sky, waiting for greatness and let life pass you by. Maybe it is a home that you desire for yourself and your family. Don't wait until you can have Michael Jackson's house before you decide to take action to get one. When I was a young Marine many of the guys in my platoon were talking about how we were all going to buy houses. When it was time for all of us to go and do it we all took different routes. There were many of us that grew up in poverty and lived in different kinds of family environments. These environments shaped the way we think. Many of the guys just felt like getting a house was just never going to happen so there were never going to try. That is just piss poor. Some of the guys bought more house than they can afford trying to present some type of image, an image of wealth. Remember that <u>wealth is</u>

what you make it and it is what you desire for yourself. So if having a house that is so big that you can barely make the payment is what you want then go ahead and do that. Or if you want a house that is so big and glamorous that you can't afford to pay the utilities, so you freeze during the winter because you cannot pay the gas bill then you go right ahead *"smart one"*. Great example you are setting for your kids.

    If you are the one that has no faith and does not believe, then go ahead and stay in that apartment for the rest of your life. Once I had a guy say to me man I can't believe your houses are so close together and that I couldn't possibly stay in your neighborhood because those houses aren't big enough and what about this, and look at that. My response to him was well I guess this neighborhood is not for you so you must be really enjoying walking up fourth flights of stairs to your apartment where your neighbor is always hitting the floor with the broom telling you to be quiet. I encouraged him to stay in that apartment because that is where that genius belongs. He would stay there for eternity if he could not afford the best house in Atlanta. The funny thing is, if we are all the same rank and the same level and all have the exact same paycheck, so it seems that we couldn't possibly be showing each other that we are wealthy by doing these things. We all do the same job and made the same amount of money exactly so, I did not believe that a big empty, cold house, with no heat as wealth. Humility and integrity will allow you to be honest with yourself and make the right decision. Don't get me wrong I am not saying that my way is the best way. There is no best way. You just have to find out what works for you and your family and tailor make a plan and program for you.

For whoever has will be given more, and whoever does not, even what he has will be taken from him.
Matthew 13:12

MULTIPLE STREAMS OF INCOME

Multiple streams of income was a big buzzword here in Atlanta when I moved here many years ago. I've seen people that will participate in every kind of pyramid scheme that came out in an effort to become wealthy. Some became network partners of this business and that business. Some would sell energy drinks some would sell any kind of item for the opportunity to succeed in business. **We must have a clear direction on what it is we came to accomplish.** I watched the schemes fall apart, one at a time.

I believe in the theory of multiple streams of income, but I do not subscribe to pyramid schemes. I am not going to pretend that I have always made the right decisions because I have done it too. If you are one of the early investors and you do it right then there is some wealth to be made. But this wealth is only made at the expense of all of the other people that are under you. I prefer to make money the old-fashioned way, work for it. Working two jobs is one way or working a job and also having a business on the side is another way. It is totally up to you what you decide but you must take action to do something.

Please bear in mind that everything that we do and every minute that we assigned to our work is a minute that we have taken away from our families. We must maintain a good work life balance. If God has called you into the ministry, your priorities must be set in order for you to accomplish the things that God has called you to do. When I was growing up all of the Preachers that I knew worked a job and then they tended to the church. Today it is different. There are more and more ministers that are making the church their priority and they have left their jobs for a career in Ministry. For the person that sees spiritual wealth and a relationship with God as, priority number one, these are the kinds of decisions that must be made and rightly so. I believe that God's business must be tended to first and I completely agree with the ministers who have chosen this route for their life, but if you are a church member, team member and you are still working a job and you cannot possibly meet the same demands on your time as the Preacher. Ministry life can be very demanding and this causes stress. Work life balance is a must. Without the right level of balance we could easily become disgruntled and dissatisfied with the work that we perform for God.

TRADE SCHOOLS VS. UNIVERSITIES

If education and training is what you need, consider attending a trade school to get a certificate or diploma and a skill that can get you employed. Don't allow yourself to be unemployed because you can't have the perfect job. Why not work at Wal-Mart? Wal-Mart is the largest employer in the world. It is larger than my company and probably larger than your company too. So why would people be ashamed to work there or why fuss and wrestle with trying to find the perfect white-collar job when they know that they haven't done the things required to get these good jobs. Wal-Mart is the kind of company that offers benefits and a consistent salary that can keep your family taking care of. I talked to tons of people that have bounced from job to job over decades of a volatile work careers; When they could've very simply gotten a job at Wal-Mart and work for 10, 15, 20, or 30 years and continue to get promoted. Consistency is great for your family. But if you would rather not work until you get the perfect job and just go ahead and stay at home and get WIC and food stamps and Social Security checks because you refuse to work if that's what you prefer. It's all up to you. Just because you couldn't go to some high-class university doesn't mean that you can't find a meaningful skill at a trade school and learn to perform your work in an excellent manner until you master your craft. Mastering your craft will make you sought after and will provide wealth.

We must continue to sharpen our skills sharpen on our pencils, master our crafts. We must continue to read and study and learn. Trade schools and universities are great places to learn but they are not the only places to learn. One of my favorite movies of all times is "Good Will Hunting." It is very simply the story of a young man who was brilliant but learned much of the knowledge that he had in the library where the library card only cost him $1.25.

Open your mind and be prepared to receive knowledge and instruction. Pray that God imparts wisdom into your life so that you can make good decisions and you will most definitely have wealth.

One big problem is that everyone thinks they're wealthy today. This prevents us from actually getting it because we have the wrong idea about what wealth is. If you ask during a survey here in the United States if a person feels that they are middle-class they will all say yes. This includes the wealthy person that is really truly financially wealthy but considers themselves only to be middle-class because they don't want to be taken advantage of and they don't want their wealth taken from them. This also includes people that are actually living in poverty and below the poverty line but consider themselves to be middle-class as well, because they desire that life whether or not they have done what it takes to get it or not. Truly I tell you, it doesn't matter what class you are what your income is and what kind of home you live in. We all have to decide what it is that we want in life and then go get it. After living a life of wealth that was attributed to a long life of crime, some men would be happy to settle for a small home that is safe and warm, where there are no hit-men looking to take them out. Wealth is different for each one of us. It is all about *perspective.*

PERSPECTIVE

The desire of man is usually dependent on their place in life currently. Maslow's Hierarchy of Needs Theory is an accurate depiction of what people need based on where they are. If you are a homeless person than what you need most is food clothing and shelter. At this point you could care less about having social status because you can't eat social status. But if you already have food clothing and shelter and you are a middle-class American than what you desire maybe retirement. A homeless man can't see retirement because he is not even sure about tomorrow. The hierarchy of needs theory is a pyramid that shows that as we achieve one level of what we need in life our desire switch to the next higher level all the way until we reach the very top where we have attained all of the material things in life that are available to be possessed. This is the place that is referred to as "Self Actualization" or "Enlightenment". This place can be reached without having the best of everything in life. To me this is all about God. Once we are done with all of the things that we have learned in this crooked world system about getting more money and more cars and more houses; we will seek a relationship with the creator. Wouldn't it be nice if we could all just seek Him?

A daily declaration is a good start for creating your plan. The Bradley's have a declaration that I use to remind me what is important and to and to restate my own faith and belief. I usually read through this about once per week as a centering mechanism to remember. From time to time, life can take a few chunks out of your self-esteem. Problems and obstacles can try to let the air out of your tires, but we must remember the motivation that we once had.

How can I write a book, work at the church, work a 9-5, create and run my own business on nights and weekends? The method is to keep moving. My declaration is about movement. It is about taking action. How do I get more done? I don't sleep. I am not suggesting this as a strategy for anyone to follow. It is my method. I am so excited about everything every day that I just have to keep going. There is so much to do. So many exciting opportunities. So much to build, and to create. We must remember the excitement that we once had for life. We have the power of life and death in the tongue. I make it my business to speak life. This is my Declaration. Instead of declaring war, I declare life. I declare greatness.

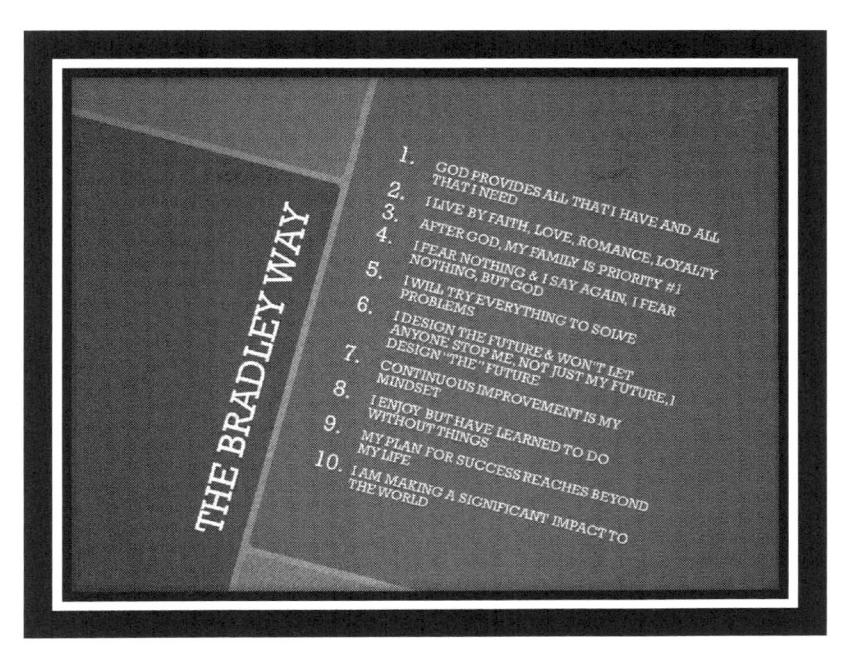

THE BRADLEY WAY

1. GOD PROVIDES ALL THAT I HAVE AND ALL THAT I NEED
2. I LIVE BY FAITH, LOVE, ROMANCE, LOYALTY
3. AFTER GOD, MY FAMILY IS PRIORITY #1
4. I FEAR NOTHING & I SAY AGAIN, I FEAR NOTHING, BUT GOD
5. I WILL TRY EVERYTHING TO SOLVE PROBLEMS
6. I DESIGN THE FUTURE & WON'T LET ANYONE STOP ME, NOT JUST MY FUTURE, I DESIGN "THE" FUTURE
7. CONTINUOUS IMPROVEMENT IS MY MINDSET
8. I ENJOY, BUT HAVE LEARNED TO DO WITHOUT THINGS
9. MY PLAN FOR SUCCESS REACHES BEYOND MY LIFE
10. I AM MAKING A SIGNIFICANT IMPACT TO THE WORLD

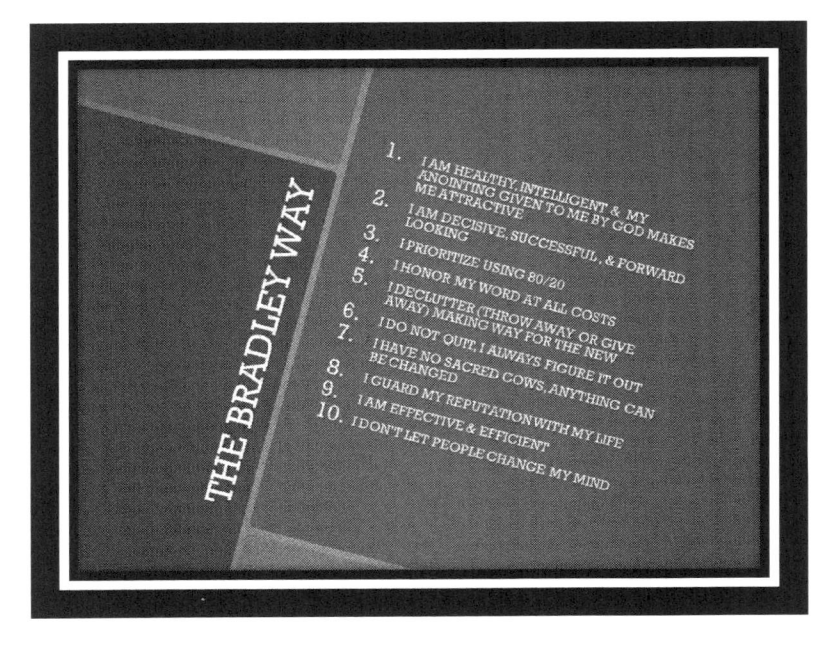

THE BRADLEY WAY

1. I AM HEALTHY, INTELLIGENT & MY ANOINTING GIVEN TO ME BY GOD MAKES ME ATTRACTIVE
2. I AM DECISIVE, SUCCESSFUL, & FORWARD LOOKING
3. I PRIORITIZE USING 80/20
4. I HONOR MY WORD AT ALL COSTS
5. I DECLUTTER (THROW AWAY OR GIVE AWAY) MAKING WAY FOR THE NEW
6. I DO NOT QUIT, I ALWAYS FIGURE IT OUT
7. I HAVE NO SACRED COWS, ANYTHING CAN BE CHANGED
8. I GUARD MY REPUTATION WITH MY LIFE
9. I AM EFFECTIVE & EFFICIENT
10. I DON'T LET PEOPLE CHANGE MY MIND

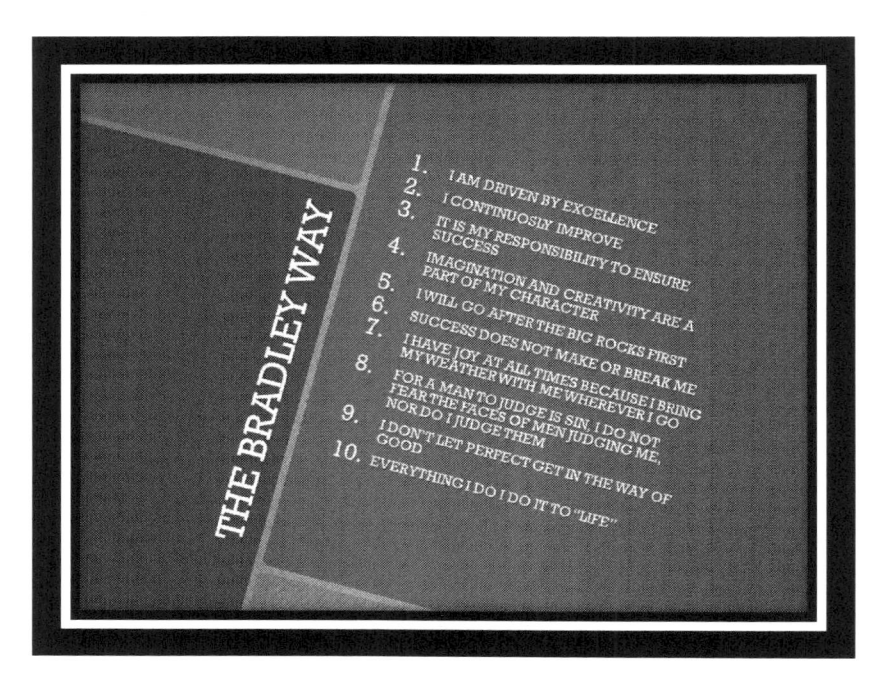

GENO BRADLEY, MBA

THE BRADLEY WAY

1. I AM DRIVEN BY EXCELLENCE
2. I CONTINUOUSLY IMPROVE
3. IT IS MY RESPONSIBILITY TO ENSURE SUCCESS
4. IMAGINATION AND CREATIVITY ARE A PART OF MY CHARACTER
5. I WILL GO AFTER THE BIG ROCKS FIRST
6. SUCCESS DOES NOT MAKE OR BREAK ME
7. I HAVE JOY AT ALL TIMES BECAUSE I BRING MY WEATHER WITH ME WHEREVER I GO
8. FOR A MAN TO JUDGE IS SIN, I DO NOT FEAR THE FACES OF MEN JUDGING ME, NOR DO I JUDGE THEM
9. I DON'T LET PERFECT GET IN THE WAY OF GOOD
10. EVERYTHING I DO I DO IT TO "LIFE"

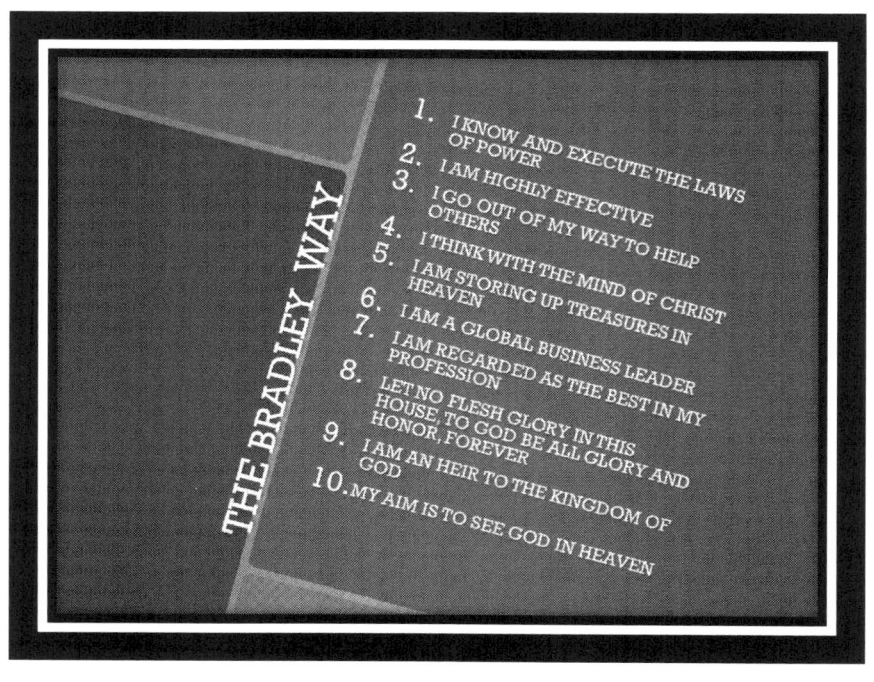

THE BRADLEY WAY

1. I KNOW AND EXECUTE THE LAWS OF POWER
2. I AM HIGHLY EFFECTIVE
3. I GO OUT OF MY WAY TO HELP OTHERS
4. I THINK WITH THE MIND OF CHRIST
5. I AM STORING UP TREASURES IN HEAVEN
6. I AM A GLOBAL BUSINESS LEADER
7. I AM REGARDED AS THE BEST IN MY PROFESSION
8. LET NO FLESH GLORY IN THIS HOUSE, TO GOD BE ALL GLORY AND HONOR, FOREVER
9. I AM AN HEIR TO THE KINGDOM OF GOD
10. MY AIM IS TO SEE GOD IN HEAVEN

IT TAKES MONEY TO MAKE MONEY

You have to be willing to spend money to get business ventures started as well. It takes money also known as "Capital" and many businesses fail because they are cash poor, but being cash poor is not the biggest problem. The biggest problem is the lack of understanding the principle of investment. Businesses must invest in their own enterprises in order to get their name out there. They need websites, business cards, advertisement, fliers, logos need to be designed, T-shirts, and uniforms. It also takes gas money to drive around to make connections.

Take the time to list it all out. What is it that you plan to attain?

- Real estate
- Cash in the bank
- Retirement savings
- Vehicles
- A business
- Net worth

The sum of all of the things that you own and all of the money that you have minus any bills that you have and any balances that you owe on your assets is your financial net worth. You don't need a fancy financial calculator or a fancy account to tell you what your net worth is. Just list it all out. And if you're not satisfied with what it is that you have at this time the make a plan to change it. If you want to change the world start with yourself you can change your world.

GBC WEALTH INDEX

Wealth Category	Score 1-10
Faith Spiritual Health	6
Giving (Obedience, Love)	9
Insurance (Property, Life)	9
Savings (Emergency, Succession) (1%=1) (2%=2) (10%=10) etc.	9
Family, Relationships, Love	5
Debt & Expenses	8
Safety & Security	8
Financial Control (Budget Accuracy)	10
Career Satisfaction (Work Type, Income)	10
Joy, Peace, Rest, (Balance)	5
Add up your Total Wealth Score	73

www.genobradley.com

KEY 5: OPERATION (ACTION ORIENTED)
Ready, Set, Go!

Ready, Set, Go!

Enough planning already, it is time to get to work. Go do it. Go do something, anything. If you have a large complex plan with many complicated parts to it, it is important to ensure that you get some small victories and accomplishments under your belt so that you can have forward momentum. It is very important that we have good plans in order to accomplish anything in life including having a wealthy and fruitful life, but at some point you half to lay your pencil down and put on your gloves and begin to work. It is time to put your hands to the plow.

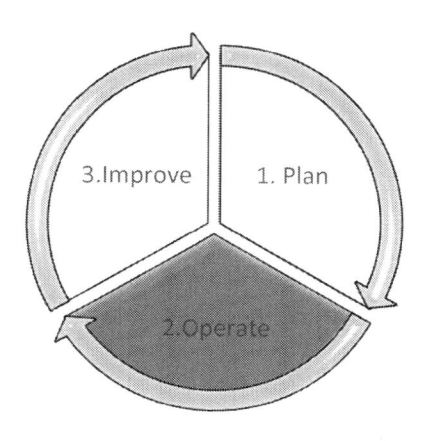

Working on financial wealth? It is time to start earning and saving and budgeting and allotting the funds in the places they should go. Working on a savings goal; and don't have a lot to save, it is time now to start saving whatever you can even if this is only a few dollars, you must begin immediately.

Start with easy techniques that will get you on your way like using the envelope method to put away few dollars each time you get paid or a piggy bank. It sounds silly but there are many people in the world that cannot save and they are convinced that they will never be able to save because they are waiting for some large pile of cash to put away. When all they need to do is start with a dollar and then two dollars and then three and then ten dollars. Continue to improve the savings amount until you're saving at the rate that matches your plan. Use automatic transfers to put money into your savings account so that it comes out automatically. Or use an allotment from your bank that automatically takes money from your net pay and deposit in a separate account. Don't wait for that pile of cash because it will never come.

Working on spiritual wealth and becoming more intimate with God? Don't wait until you think that you are holy enough to come into the midst of God because you will never be holy enough. The Bible says that we have all fallen short of the glory. This includes you and it also includes every person that has ever gone to church. It also includes every preacher and teacher and evangelist. They have all fallen short as well and the Good ones will actually admit this to you in their open confessions because they have already mastered the understanding of the imperfection of man and the perfection of God. It is very simple to start with the Scriptures and start reading your Bible immediately. You don't have to start memorizing the Scriptures, just start reading them.

"Good things may come to those who wait, but it will only be the few things left over by those who hustle."
Abraham Lincoln

The Bible is large and it may be intimidating if you are a fearful person. Stop being a baby and start with one small passage of scripture. Read the scripture and then pray to God to help you to understand it. It is all you need to get started. Don't have a prayer life? Start praying immediately. You do not have to wait until you can do magnificent, outstanding, eloquent, prayers of enormous verbose, ineffectual words. Just start talking to God and tell him how you feel and tell him that you believe in him and ask him to teach you all of the rest and God will find a way to get the knowledge that you need into your head. More than likely he will place man and woman of God that he trust on assignment to assist.

This is a part of the action cycle. "Plan, **Operate**, Improve". What are you waiting for to go change the world? If you want things to change, start with yourself. Enough procrastination already, it's time to step into action. This is "operation".

BE ACTION ORIENTED!

We are all oriented to one thing or another. Whether it is oriented towards procrastination, or oriented towards lies, or oriented towards blaming others, or oriented towards action. Be Action Oriented! Action speaks louder than words.

SELF-STARTER

Be a Self-Starter. Don't be the type of individual that needs help all the time. Don't be the kind of person that is always looking for a hand up. It is okay to get a hand up and assistance along the way and allow others to invest into us but don't be so reliant on it that we are paralyzed by inaction and the inability to think for ourselves. We must have initiative. If we don't then we are just like those little yellow things on the movie "despicable me". Just little minions. I have worked with many different people in different places in life that were completely paralyzed by the inability to think for themselves and it is disgusting and repulsive to be around people like this. They show no initiative whatsoever and have to ask a question before they do every single little thing that they do. The leaders that they have are probably also sick of the fact that they cannot think for themselves and they wished that they had individuals on their teams that were more capable. There must be something inside you that is motivating you and driving you into destiny. Think.

PROCRASTINATION

We must break the cycles of procrastination. Procrastination is the enemy of action. Do not put off until tomorrow something that can be done today. This happens a lot with people because they are still in the planning phase and still thinking of how they will get things done and still making a very long list of all the stuff that they need and all of the help that they need before they can start. Well I believe that this is nonsensical. This is how we end up in the poorhouse. At some point we have to stop planning and then "go do it". So what! Your plan isn't perfect. It doesn't matter. Just start moving in that direction and you will have gained some ground and taken some territory. But if you disagree then procrastination is what you prefer. Feel free to procrastinate all you want in the name of planning and preparation and you will get nothing accomplished. Looking up at the sky will not make anything happen for you. So go get it and go do it right now. *Get Motivated, Be Inspired, And Then Inspire Someone Else.*

"*The soul of the sluggard craves and gets nothing, while the soul of the diligent is richly supplied.*"
Proverbs 13:14

KEY 6: INFINITY
The Pencil Sharpener

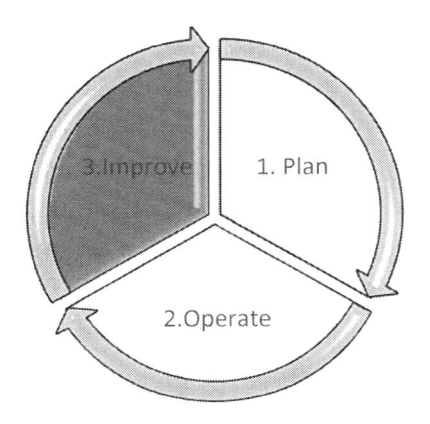

I Can't Stop!

No matter what kind of wealth it is that you are seeking and no matter what it is that is important to you in life, you will no doubt have to work very hard in order to get anything that is worth having. And once you have achieved one point it is simply a connection to the next point. One thing that is consistent among successful people is that they never stop improving. The most successful people in life, be it financial or otherwise, have one common thread between them: Once they achieve one goal they set another goal to achieve. This is *"infinity"*.

During my work as a business executive I have employed an interwoven strategy of continuous improvement in every endeavor. I have learned the theory of continuous improvement both in formal schools like Georgia Tech and Kennesaw State University but I have also learned the strategies tools and techniques of continuous improvement from individuals that I have worked with. The best leaders that I have had believed deeply to their core that continuous improvement is the only strategy. Good business executives make it a mission in life to keep getting better in every aspect of their life and this is also evident in their personal lives.

The strategy of continuous improvement is also very helpful in establishing goals in the first place. Once you understand that we will constantly improve we can stop trying to make everything perfect before we get started. Make a good solid plan work your plan and have improvement along the way as a part of the plan. If you wait until the plan is perfect you will never get started, because there are no perfect plans. Plans are nothing but planning is critical. I heard a saying once that if you want to make God laugh tell him your plans. I believe that this is not to say that we shouldn't plan, but more importantly it is to say that we must understand that there will be many changes along the way.

In my spiritual life it is imperative that I wake up every morning thanking God for allowing me to wake up and knowing that I must continue to strive for excellence. Knowing that I am not there yet. Knowing that I have not arrived. Knowing that we have all fallen short of the glory of God, and with that knowledge I must continue to press on. If there was ever a point where a man believed that he had arrived he would immediately stop getting better. He would stop growing. He would stop getting closer to God. No matter how good or moral I have become it will never be enough for me. I must continue to strive daily for the excellence of Christ. I will not allow vanity or pride to set into my mind and allow me to be swindled into a philosophy that will end in destruction.

In financial matters we must understand also that the very basic theory of inflation is enough for us to continue to grow our portfolios. It's enough for us to know as a matter of fact that we must continue to invest, that we must continue to find ways to have our assets earn interest. Simply having money is not enough. As inflation continues to rise it would only take a matter of years before the money that you have is worth nothing because the prices of everything continue to rise. So in financial matters and managing financial assets we must continue to improve and look for new strategies to invest.

As we all work at our jobs and our businesses we must continue to find a way to get better at performing our tasks and rendering our services. If we are not moving forward then we are moving backwards. The entire world is constantly moving including the earth. As the world turns on its axis and the seasons change, as more people are born and more ideas are being birthed; there are new strategies and new competitors constantly emerging into your business environment. There are new coworkers that are being hired that are gunning for your job, so you must continue to find ways to improve your work. We must continue to find ways to reduce costs as business owners. The cost of materials and supplies to conduct our work continues to rise so if we don't constantly find more efficient ways to render our services and to deliver the goods you will very quickly find out that what used to be a profit will turn into breaking even and then it will turn into a loss. Do not allow yourself to remain stagnant in one place with one method for eternity, because if you do, you might find yourself left out in the cold or left behind with the times. It's very important that we think outside the box at new ways to get things done, and new ways to get from one point to another, new ways to communicate and new ways of working with one another through teamwork.

In our family lives we must also strive to continue to get better. You must continue to find new ways to appreciate the people that are around us we cannot continue the same routines day in and day out. Continue to surprise your spouse with compliments and gifts and activities that keep her interested and attracted. We must continue to do all of the things to maintain our love that we did when we were dating, when we were trying to get that love. We must continue to find new and better ways to train our children. We must constantly stay connected to the environments that are children go out into. We must understand the technologies and methodologies that they are using in the schools and in their social environment so that we can protect them from predators. Anything that your children are involved in that you are not involved in or that you don't understand is a grave risk. How can you protect your children from something that you don't understand? And to think that you will keep them from it is naïve. Continue to remain sharp and be vigilant. Go to your children's school and be involved with the teachers, be involved with your child's learning process be involved with their school activities, spend time talking with them and find out what's happening with them and what's new in their lives.

If you simply dictate to your children what to do and that's all you do: you'll soon find out that you don't even know who your child is, and I don't need that. As soon as they are independent enough to make their own choices, the lifestyle that they choose for themselves will be something that is completely foreign to you because you never got to actually know them. It is amazing to me how many people have finally figured parenting out once they become grandparents. Every grandparent wants to go and tell the parents now that you should spend more time talking to your child and that you should be more patient and that you should spend more time lecturing and teaching them and getting to know them then just beating them. However that same grandparent beat the hell out of their child when they were the parent. What why wait until your time is done and gone before you figure this out. Furthermore, please don't be unwise in your decision to let someone who doesn't have children tell you how to raise your child. I don't care how wise they seem to be, they have no earthly idea what it means to be a parent. Don't allow someone that is not married to speak into your marriage and tell you how to handle your spouse. This is insane.

Do you know why they have scoreboards during sporting events? It is so that you will know the score. Don't you want to know whether you're winning or losing? If not you will be playing a never ending game with no objective. This is also the reason why the statistics are kept very accurately in sports. So why on earth would you not keep statistics in mind in managing your business affairs and your personal affairs and your financial affairs? What about your spiritual affairs. Knowledge is power. It is the power to understand so that you can take action. Proactive operation is the ability to correct and adjust in places where you see that you have fallen short of the mark. Keeping track of your financial affairs and your savings rate? If they are not on track then adjust your plan. Are you making donations to your local church or charity but what you give is not quite measuring up to what you think you can give, then adjust your plan. Not spending enough time with your wife or your husband or your children; then adjust everything in your life around your family. In order to know whether things are going the way they were planned you must first to have a plan, and then it is critical that you measure. Without measuring you won't know.

"When you're writing and, it gets a little harder to do, sharpen your pencil."   - Geno Bradley

KEY 7: HUMILTY
A Servant's Heart

One day you're on top, the next day you are not, so be careful how you do business and how you attend to your business affairs. We must have a set of standards that we abide by. These morals and values must be the guiding principles that provide the boundaries for our daily life, our personal life, and our business affairs. If we are not careful how we treat others, then someday we may find ourselves on the other end of that stick.

Whatever amount of wealth that you have and no matter what type of wealth it is, without humility you will not keep it. Humility is what keeps men from becoming prideful. It is essential for a good life. Anything and any area where we become prideful and becomes a risk for us. We are at risk because, we no longer see our own transgressions or missteps or mistakes. Pride prevents us from being honest with ourselves about our own abilities. It keeps us from giving credit to others where credit is due. It prevents us from being gracious and showing appreciation and gratitude to those who have assisted us along the way and to those who have made great investments into our lives and our futures.

We must all be honest about the things that we have, the things that we desire, and our own abilities and inabilities. No one wants a star player with a bad attitude on their team. An NFL wide receiver that I will not name was a very talented player but could not remain on any team for long because he was not good in the locker room. He was not good at building others up. With all of the talent that he had, in the end it did not amount to the full potential that it could have because he lacked humility.

Kobe Bryant is one of my favorite basketball players of all time because of his skill but not because of his attitude. The difference between him and Michael Jordan is that, Michael Jordan made everyone around him better and he made the guys around him feel like they were a part of the team and that they were part of the success. Michael Jordan had no problem sharing the stage or complementing his guys for the contributions that they made to get the win. It is my own personal belief that Kobe Bryant was physically more adept and talented that Michael Jordan. He could jump higher, and he could shoot better, but he was not a good leader. Michael Jordan was an excellent leader and this is the reason that he is regarded as the best player of all times. It has been said by many that Kobe Bryant wanted to try and surpass the accomplishments of Michael Jordan but it will never happen because he lacks humility.

There will be many people that disagree with the statement that I made about the sports players and many of the other comments that I made in this book, and you are all entitled to your own opinion. This is mine. You don't have to agree with the details of my opinion in order to get a true understanding of my point. The point and the principle of the matter is not about sports or about the players it is about ***humbling yourself***.

A prideful husband may not appreciate his wife in the right manner prideful, children may not properly address a respect their parents. A prideful coworker will not acknowledge the accomplishments of their fellow coworkers. A prideful business owner may not give proper respect to those who have paved the way for them. Just in the same manner that prideful slave owners did not give proper honor and respect to God and treat their servants with respect. I am in no way condoning slavery at any point in history or in any way but God was well aware of the fact that men would enslave each other, into this and God very clearly in the Bible gave specific instructions on how slaves were to be treated and that after a certain time that they were to be released. Pride prevented any of this from happening. Every man and every woman will have to give account for every action that they have taken during their life and that includes you and I.

> *"Pride comes before destruction"*
> *Proverbs 16:18*

Pride prevents men from giving honor to God for breath in their lungs, fort the roof over their head, and for the families that we have. Pride prevents men from giving honor to God for every accomplishment and instead at times we will take credit for our own inventions and our accomplishments and say that it was our intelligence that made it happen.

A servant's heart is imperative. It is very important that we learn to play our position. Because whatever team member we become will be the same type of team members that we will inherit. If you are a "know it all" that has to have everything done their own way or, the type of person to disrespect their leaders and talks bad about them behind their back, then one day when you are in charge and in a position of authority you will have people that are on your team that will treat you the exact same way.

If you are an inmate in a correctional facility, humility will be the ticket out of the joint. When it comes time to evaluate whether or not you will be released for good behavior or released early for parole; they will take an account of your activity with the other inmates and with the guards. If you have attacked guards over and over again and hurled insults and spit at the warden then you will very likely do your entire sentence and more. And if they get an opportunity to charge you with any additional crimes while you were in, they will do so and make sure that you stay in that jail. A lack of humility will keep you incarcerated because you failed to honor the laws of the land and were convicted. That same lack of humility will keep you incarcerated for longer because you failed to be rehabilitated and show remorse and humility. Don't be silly enough to think that I believe that jails can rehabilitate men. That is not what I am driving at. My point is simply that you will be evaluated based on your behavior towards others and we must learn how to play the game. For someone who is incarcerated "Freedom" is the wealth.

We will continue to learn the same lessons over and over again until we pass the tests. As young members of the US military we are in constant turmoil and trouble because of the way that we either respect or disrespect our leaders. You can be restricted to the barracks and not allowed to go out and have fun on the weekends which restricts your freedom and liberty. This freedom and liberty is a form of wealth that we are having stripped away from us because of our lack of ability to show respect. Maybe you do not value the freedom to go out on your own or the liberty to travel where you please and if this applies to you then just go ahead and continue being the disrespectful little monster that you are. You will continue the same cycle until you get it or until you get thrown in the brig and lose a stripe. If you ever get this lesson "down-packed" then at some point you will be promoted and become a military leader. Additionally, you better hope that you don't receive a disrespectful little brat just like you use to be. If you do, just remember who you were and that you also did this same bad behavior once. Remembering where you came from will give you a level of humility that will keep you from being overbearing to these younger military members, or younger workers at your job, or younger congregation members in your church, or younger family members. It applies to every situation. The same situation that I am describing to you is also evident in family life. Disrespectful little children will continue to be on punishment and lose privileges because of their lack of humility.

Judgment is reserved for God, so please reserve all of your personal thoughts to yourself. Try to have your mind changed so that you can be open to others their feelings and their ideas. Be open to the fact that no man is perfect so that you don't attempt to crucify everyone that you know for not being perfect.

If you are close to your leaders, whether it is in business or in church, or in a fraternity, or in family, then you have been privileged to very personal information. During your time spent with people that are in authority you will have seen their weaknesses, because every man has weaknesses. Whether it is your boss at work, or your parents, or your preacher at the church, or if it is your favorite music, and television celebrities, they are always on display and being watched by all. This is the kind of thing that can cause trouble especially if the leader has a lack of integrity. *We all make mistakes in life.*

The differences for these leaders and celebrities and people in authority is: It is much easier for them to be caught and then put on display. We make spectacles of them because we have found out about their mistakes. Humility and a servant's heart can prevent man from judging one another and crucifying one another. When I see some person that is being blasted on the news for doing something stupid the only thing that I can say is that I pray that this person remains encouraged throughout this matter and I pray that this person knows God and just praying to God for Him to have his way with the situation. Be honest, if your life was a reality TV show and people had spy cameras all over the place what would they say about you and your life? Would they see you digging in your nose and then flicking it on the wall? Will they see you cussing out your wife and children? Would they see you run every stop sign you come to? Would they see your road rage and how irate that you become when you're driving?

Would they be able to understand that this is the same person that smiles and nods and is very pleasant in certain situations? Well ladies and gentlemen, we all have issues and my point here is that no man is to judge another. You should only continue to reconcile your soul and your activities and all of your actions and every word that you have ever spoken and everyplace that you have ever gone to with God. It is between you and him. If you don't, it is impossible to maintain any form of wealth. If you ever gain wealth for any reason then without humility it is impossible to keep it. As soon as you hit a bump in the road it will all be stripped away from you because that is the way that you have treated others.

KEY 8: INTEGRITY
It Matters How You Win

What is the guiding principle for your life? What are your morals and values? Does your company have a set of morals and values that they have ascribed to? If you want your own business, have you taken the time to write out your mission statement to say what it is that you believe and what you aim to accomplish?

It doesn't matter what your model says, there are several values models that are in use in Americas corporations today. If your company does not have a set of values, you had better take the time to write it out. Using God's principles in business and in personal matters is always the best strategy to employ. Bible says that if we do not honor God and his commandments that everyman will do what is right in his own eyes. This means very simply that today what you believe to be right is one thing and you will more than likely change that very thing at some point in the future. You may be susceptible to changing with the wind because you have no standard. Ensure that there is a set of standards and principles that govern your life.

It matters very much how we win. It matters how we our earn profits. If you became the head of a successful corporation that earned billions of dollars in profit but you found out that you exploited people in the process and that you destroyed lives and families and that you abused your workers, you are responsible for the outcome.

Integrity is making sure that you do the right thing even when no one is looking. Don't take advantage of the situation just because you can or, just because you will not be caught. Be sure to conduct your affairs in an ethical manner because you will reap what you sow. In respect to integrity we must do a self-check. Did I step on anyone in order to move up, or, to move ahead? Did I take from anyone? Did I hurt anyone to get here? I am not here to condemn you, I am not here to point fingers. I am simply offering a very easy reminder to do a complete evaluation of yourself and your activities to see if any of it was dishonorable.

If you are one of the people who are honest with himself or herself and you have taken a look back at your life and you have realized that some of the things that you've done were dishonorable then you need to reconcile it. The debt needs to be repaid. The bad deed needs to be redeemed and your soul needs to be cleaned. This is part of the reason why some of the people that our money-wealthy in the world will never be completely happy. It is simple because they ignored all of the other forms of wealth and all of the other things in life that are important.

Having good integrity enhances your character and makes you a better man or woman. It makes you more trustworthy. This way God continue to bless you with more and more. A sports team that cheats to get to victory or a businessman that breaks the law to get ahead is the same thing. They are both dishonest and God will reconcile this behavior. It is better to acknowledge your own issues and the things that *we* need to improve on, because if we don't then it just might be reconciled for us because, what goes around comes around. Reconcile it, Give back, and Share the Equity.

> *"For what does it profit a man to gain the whole world and then lose his own soul?"*
>
> ***Mark 8:36***

:EPILOGUE

The Wealthy House

Hopefully, you have learned at least one new fact or new scripture that you didn't know before. Or, maybe some passage of text helped to change your perspective on wealth. If at least one thing stays with you, then that is enough for me to claim victory. In the beginning of the book, I asked what you would do with your last two dollars. After reading this, has your answer changed? What's your new answer? Any of the material stands out? Write it below:

_____

_____

_____

_____

_____

_____

_____

_____

_____

_____

So what was my rant all about? In the end, every man will have to define for himself what is most important to him and what he is willing to do to get it. There is no "one way" to do it. Choose your own way. Make a plan and then make it work. In a wealthy house you will find each of the 8 Keys in full operation.

For me, it is God and then my family in that order and I will do anything for them. This is my reasoning for using scriptural references throughout this book. How much will I give for it? How much will I invest into them? How far will I go? I will go to the ends of the earth and I will stop at nothing. I will pray without ceasing all of the days of my life and I will love my family they best way that I know how. Having those two things makes me wealthy, even if I never make another dime. All of the other stuff is just the gravy on top. I say good morning to people and lots of people say it to me as well. Most of the time I respond with, *"It's a good life."*

This book is my strategy. It is my plan. It is my way of life. I don't have to try to do this, because it is who I am. I do not consider myself to be perfect in any of the categories of this strategy, but remember if we are getting it right, then we are not waiting until the plan is perfect, or waiting until the behavior is perfect to make an improvement, or to take action. I will continue to pray to God for the *Wisdom*. I will *Give* until it hurts, I will study and practice to gain *Competency.* I will plan my *Strategy*. I will work - *Operate* the strategy. I will measure to see how I have done, and then I will *improve.* I will also strive with everything in me to live my life with *Humility* and *Integrity.*

If I only had two dollars left, I would put split it with God. I would put one dollar in the church offering basket, and I would use the other to buy a box of moon pies. Moon Pies & Little Debbie cakes may not seem like the best choice, but 12 of them comes in the box, so I could share with anyone that was near. "Love the Lord your God with all your heart, and your entire mind, and all your soul, and love your fellow man as yourself".

As I leave you, I ask for consideration in 2 important matters before you close the pages to this book and place it on the shelf. The first consideration is: that you pick it up again someday to see if you feel differently. I am confident that as we age our perspective changes. The second consideration is to take 2 minutes of your life to consider in reflection this one statement, which is more important to me than any other words I have written: *If God was the only thing that you had, would it be enough?*

> "*If God was the only thing that you had,
> Would it be enough?*"

End Notes

- The Holy Bible
- Dr. Rhonda E. Travitt; Restoring the Years Global Ministries
- http://dictionary.reference.com/browse/wisdom?s=t
- http://dictionary.reference.com/browse/knowledge?s=t
- http://www.movemequotes.com/top-10-take-action-quotes/
- http://www.census.gov/content/dam/Census/library/publications/2014/demo/p60-249.pdf
- Black Girls Rock, BET
- My Future, My Education Speech, President Obama September 8, 2009
- bleacherreport.com/...to-mlbs-all-time-hit-leaders
- http://www.baseball-almanac.com/hitting/hihits1.shtml
- http://cmgww.com/baseball/cobb/
- http://www2.ucsc.edu/whorulesamerica/power/wealth.html
- Movie: Good Will Hunting
- Maslow's Hierarchy of Needs

:About The Author

Geno Bradley is a dedicated husband, father and a devout Disciple of Jesus Christ. His professional career began in the United States Marine Corp where he served for 11 years matriculating through various units within the service. Geno graduated from St. Leo University in 2006 with a Bachelor's Degree in Business Administration. With a passion for education and learning, he graduated in 2009 from Kennesaw State University with a Career Growth Masters of Business Administration degree. In 2004, Geno opened, The Geno Bradley Company providing a host of business and financial services to his clients.

Geno is married to the love of his life, Latrisa and together they parent one daughter and currently reside in the Metro-Atlanta, Georgia area.

For more information on Geno Bradley and Geno Bradley Co. visit www.genobradley.com

GBC WEALTH INDEX
WWW.GENOBRADLEY.COM

Wealth Category	Score 1-10
Faith Spiritual Health	
Giving (Obedience, Love)	
Insurance (Property, Life)	
Savings (Emergency Saving, Succession Planning, Retirement) (1%=1) (2%=2) (10%=10) etc. Give yourself 1% for each percent of your gross income that you save.	
Family, Relationships, Love	
Debt & Expenses	
Safety & Security	
Financial Control (Budget Accuracy)	
Career Satisfaction (Work Type, Income)	
Joy, Peace, Rest, (Balance)	
Total Score	

Geno Bradley Co.

GBCATL
Est. 1978
Loyalty · Respect
★ ★ ★ ★
Merchandising & Production

Made in the USA
Charleston, SC
16 June 2015